A Mother

Is an

Intellectual

Thing

———

ALSO BY KIMBERLY GREY

Systems for the Future of Feeling
The Opposite of Light

A Mother
Is an
Intellectual
Thing

Essays

Kimberly
Grey

A Karen & Michael Braziller Book
PERSEA BOOKS / NEW YORK

Persea Books, Inc.
90 Broad Street
New York, New York 10004

Library of Congress Cataloging-in-Publication Data

Names: Grey, Kimberly, 1985– author.
Title: A mother is an intellectual thing : essays / Kimberly Grey.
Description: New York : Persea Books, 2023. | Includes bibliographical references. | Summary: "Ingenious out of necessity, A Mother Is an Intellectual Thing centers around the scapegoating and exile of the author by her mother. In these essays, Kimberly Grey harnesses her formidable intellectual and creative resources to create coherence for an unstable, traumatized self. To do so, she calls on-beseeches-dozens of brilliant thinkers and artists for help, among them Etel Adnan, Roland Barthes, John Cage, Anna Freud, Mina Loy, Elaine Scarry, Gertrude Stein, and Simone Weil. Grey's engagement with these figures (and many others) is part of her effort to stabilize, if not fully comprehend, the inconceivability of her maternal banishment. By thinking her pain rather than feeling it, Grey becomes an expert witness to her own trauma, a ponderer of motherhood even as her identity as daughter has been rescinded"—Provided by publisher.
Identifiers: LCCN 2023037014 | ISBN 9780892555758 (paperback)
Subjects: LCSH: Motherhood. | Mothers and daughters.
Classification: LCC HQ759 .G77 2023 | DDC 306.874/3—dc23/eng/20230822
LC record available at https://lccn.loc.gov/2023037014

Book design and composition by Rita Lascaro
Typeset in Goudy Old Style
Manufactured in the United States of America. Printed on acid-free paper.

Contents

For a Tear is an Intellectual Thing,
And the Sigh is the sword of an Angel King,
And the bitter groan of the Martyr's woe
Is an Arrow from the Almighty's bow.

–WILLIAM BLAKE

Mère, pleure
Moi, je pense.
Mother, weep
While I think.

—STÉPHANE MALLARMÉ

INITIO

"Unable to remember, the beginner guesses," writes Lyn Hejinian. She writes other things, too, about the sun shining and little beats of time and low-lying blue. In the new true mirrors, you can see a woman standing at a door. There, at dawn, is doubt, a sun-drenched line of strangers, and a whirlpool turning a crowd. As such, I arrive at the beginning. I will try to give you a synopsis, though it is not, as Hejinian asserts, even possible.

Nonetheless, nonetheless. I think she was right when she wrote, "It really is melancholy being a beginner." There are sequences and sentences, and they are sometimes less playful and more aching. When I begin, I think, *am I beginning?* I look around and I, too, pursue. When Hejinian writes, "I'm beginning, and thinking that I think myself launched into something," I am also being launched. All that has occurred does so in many ways, but the past has not yet withdrawn from a beginner. Hejinian wrote that, but I've made the two distinct sentences into one, and by doing so, make it mine to begin again. The tracks that have made themselves, make themselves, you see?

Perhaps the most important thing that Hejinian writes is that "One cannot dream until one begins." I read and read, repeat and repeat, until eventually I bend. I bend myself down all the way, all the way down to sleep, to sleep I bend to sentences. I bend to the question, to all questions, to this one, to write, to have written, to dream: am I meant to begin—again and again—or to end and end and end this thinking?

*

Here is the problem a poem can't answer: my mother
is rife with erasure. She disappears slowly like a limb
lost fastly. Logic has no place here. Language will
replace her leaving and then it will also break. I promise
I am awake on the page as I was not awake in life.
If I remember her face at all now, it is that it was shapely,
and in my dreams, a summing of angles and degrees.
She was almost really there. But a mother left me just to
leave, and, in her going, left a shape of cruelty as round
as a sun burned deep in my head. (Yes, each moment
of learning is a new turn). Or take what Stevens said,

A Mother

Is an

Intellectual

Thing

———

DISLOCATION

A mother can dislocate you.

No one tells you this, so I will do the telling.

For years I've wandered around in separations; a legless knee floating in distinctive clicks. Dislocation, by definition, can be a biological or geographical occurrence. Scholars describe it as a "disruption" or "displacement." Doctors say "luxation." I understand it best in two common ways:

A person can be fully intact, though they are dislocated from their country or home of origin.

Or a person can sleep in the soft bed they were born to, their body pulled apart like a splayed doll.

Dis-, a Latin prefix, meaning "apart," "asunder," "away," "utterly."

We all come to the world needing a location. To be located. This is the main argument for taking a lover. *They feel like home*, one might say, meaning, when I'm with them I feel tethered to something. And location, for the time being, a place of settlement. We'd all like our locations to feel permanent. We'd like to think permanency is dictated by how hard we hold on.

A mother is a first country. A first location. She is there all around us literally and then there all around us metaphorically. We can't conceive of the world without her.

It is her, entire. She, Motherworld.

*

When I think of being dislocated *by* the mother, I lose the capacity to think. When I think of being dislocated *from* her, I think that I am like a train car now separated from its engine; thing that pulls you along through the wilderness, through beauty and danger; mother-engine choosing its direction. Poet Li-Young Lee writes this metaphor using another kind of vehicle:

> "Good boat, first boat, old boat, Mother,
> my first night with you lasted nine months.
> Our second night together is the rest of my life."

i. *The First Dislocation*

It's physical. It comes at birth. The bodies are one and then not-one. The multiplication of it doesn't matter. It's the subtraction, the un-ness, that creates disturbance. Something to love now, a mother might think. Though, contrary to all popular belief, this is not always true. A person is created using her body and that person is of new body. There's a rupture in perceived ownership, perceived location.

Otto Rank wrote of this concept in his book *Das Trauma der Geburt* (The Trauma of Birth). A colleague of Sigmund Freud, Rank wrote of being "born into trauma." He believed that the birthing process is the beginning of all suffering and wrote that the separation from the mother is not just physical, but also psychic, violent and that this movement away from attachment and union is one's first experience with aloneness and fear. According to Rank, this initial moment of anxiety is a blueprint for every future anxiety we feel. But he is referring to the trauma endured by the baby. Not the mother. Whose job is it to think about the mother?

The little body leaves the mother-body. Wayward and away. A dislocation by nature. Meaning it is natural. This is supposed to happen.

ii. *The Second Dislocation*

Detachment is healthy, necessary. The child grows and naturally moves through the world.

The mother must allow it.

Adolescence is a further dislocation. Psychoanalyst Edward Bowlby explained this necessity. Born in London to a wealthy family, Bowlby spent most of his childhood with a nanny. A substitute mother, he'd say. Maternal deprivation became an obsession and, thus, the basis for his attachment theory.

The theory states that an infant comes into the world pre-programmed to form attachments to others, most specifically their mother. The infant responds to the mother's ability (or inability) to provide a secure base for exploring the world. How a child attaches to its mother becomes a platform to which all their future relationships depend on, determines how a human will respond when hurt, separated, threatened, or wrong(ed).

By adolescence, the child experiences a rate of rapid development cognitively, biologically, emotionally.

The mother must allow it.

The child explores the world for the first time as an autonomous being: a natural transition to adulthood. Psychologist Carl E. Pickhardt wrote that this process is more painful for the mother than the child.

He calls it "daring to let go."

ii.   *The Third Dislocation*

It is unnatural, the third dislocation. The mother malfunctions, decides the child is no longer necessary, has grown and betrayed her, doesn't fit her needs as the other children do. And so, she discards the child like an old, unpaired sock. An excruciating dislocation. The child is left wandering: apart, asunder, away, utterly like a goat across the scape.

Because of this the child opens up language, tries to fix the mother. The child must become an I; shift her narrative distance to get closer to her mother. But when she does this, everything becomes metaphor:

Like a carburetor, she is flooded. I wait, open choke, crank
the throttle wide open. There's always a violent answer
to which this language applies. I push the pedal down
to the floor, try and try to engage her. Small shot of ether
down the throat. Use a screwdriver in case she backfires,
protect my hands. She doesn't sputter, doesn't make
a sound. I kneel and stand, kneel and stand. It must be
something electrical, crossed wires. A hot engine of sobbing
I am, the first rule, not giving in. She's the deadest kind
of battery, wreckage in the past must have ruined, and
now it strikes me that I am, in these fumes, also wrecked.
She is a crucial car, a futile car, an old combustion of
necessary fuel, brutal love, and faulty sparks. I turn
her off and on, off and on—but the mother won't start.

"To turn a page without moving into a new life," writes Etel Adnan. Dailiness is at the heart of every conflict. Mine is not a war, but still—destructive total. I wish it were visible, this frozen state of being. I want time to move me like Adnan's verbs. Can the infinitive start me? Make me go? Can the "to" link itself to its verb and make a little train of movement and take me away; far and forward, to and to, the places that are apart from my mother?

[To cross the Golden Gate.]
—ADNAN

To think you have made it to another world.

To look back at the city's flashes.

To see fog as atmospheric erasure.

To ignore what wells in you.

To think the red beams are actually burnt brown.

To never claim anything as sound.

To know so many have jumped.

To try to find a new way to sing.

To not bother combing your hair in the wind.

IDEATION

To mark a thing in its becoming is my intention. How in California, the salt ponds, look, from above, like arresting maps I once followed to find where I begin.

California: where I moved to when I moved away from the mother. I thought distance would create a needfulness, that I'd become a *sine qua non.* I wanted to feel what Toni Morrison said she felt: "the pleasure of being necessary." But I did not yet understand understanding.

*

If there was a map for understanding the mother, it might look like this:

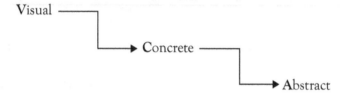

VISUAL: She's tall but not . . . so thin and yes much like my . . . red, short and long . . . and her hands . . . yes . . . likes to . . . turn away from . . . her favorite color, I'm not sure . . . I barely remember . . . some gradual and small expressions on her face of . . . immense though, immense . . .

This visual conjuring does not work. So I try what's next.

CONCRETE: She's a woman who loved . . . is still . . . it's been years . . . I can't know . . . what surprised me . . . the alterations and . . . their magnifying . . . I try to magnify . . . the physical thing of her . . . time bites at . . . what she told me . . . saying . . .

I could not attach any image to her. And so, slept to avoid waking, slept to avoid pain and light and all literal interpretations of her: photographs, smells, voices with her sound. Slept a year away.

Then I woke, as Jacques Lacan wrote, "from a short nap by knocking at my door just before I actually woke. With this impatient knocking I had already formed a dream, a dream that manifested to me something other than knocking. And when I awake, it is in so far as I reconstitute my entire representation around this knocking—this perception—that I am aware of it."

The mother doesn't know what I know. Lacks the awareness. I want her to be minimized in my mind's irascible bending. I want her to be translated into the abstract.

ABSTRACT: This is my thinking as it occurs: the thing's thingness must step away so that I may grasp it—as I haven't been able to before.

Lacan: "So I began to dream under the effect of the knocking which is, to all appearances, what woke me."

*

I have read from Freud's *Die Traumdeutung*, over and over, the dream of the burning child, trying to decipher the true moment of the realization of loss: the dream or the waking?

> A father had been watching beside his child's sick-bed for days and nights on end. After the child had died, he went into the next room to lie down, but left the door open so that he could see from his bedroom into the room in which his child's body was laid out, with tall candles standing round it. An old man had been engaged to keep watch over it and sat beside the body murmuring prayers. After a few hours' sleep, the father had a dream that his child was standing beside his bed, caught him by the arm and said, 'Father, don't you see I'm burning?' He woke up, noticed a bright glare of light from the next room, hurried into it and found that the old watchman had dropped off to sleep and that the wrappings and one of the arms of his beloved child's dead body had been burned by a lighted candle that had fallen on them.

To Lacan's question, "What is it that wakes the sleeper? Is it not, in the dream, another reality?" I'm inclined to answer *yes, a cruel one.*

—the reality that Freud describes thus   —*Dass das Kind an seinem Bette steht,*   that the child is near her bed,   *ihn am Arme fast,*   takes her by the arm and whispers to her

7

reproachfully,   *und ihm vorwurfsvoll zurant: Mutter siehst du*
den nicht,   Mother, can't you see,   *dass ich verbrenne,*
that I am burning?

REALIZATION

The problem is, I am not real. These words circle my mind like an abstract crown, not quite birds or thorns, and not so much to mock me, but to make sure I don't lose my place in reality. Words I have now to apply to a self I've never fully understood. These words, that sometimes scatter themselves like clouds low-lit by a coming rain, not understandable in their ominous form but present, and moving slightly away to clear a frame for a new way of thinking. But what? I am always moving toward knowledge, but never actually arriving.

How many seas have I stood before, face-forward, trying to determine the exactness of external beauty? How many sunsets over a mountain range? How many glances out of the house's framed window?

What is real is the clouds, I know for sure.

Even when I fly through them, the plane shuddering in its newfound enclosure, even if just briefly, I feel I am experiencing reality: water vapor condensed to form tiny water droplets suspended in air shaped like, well, whatever you see in that given moment: horse, flower, fist.

"I am not real" feels like the truest exclamation I've found to relate my experience of life. And it did not begin when I lost the mother in early adulthood, but early in childhood. I remember being six years old and thinking *I am not real like my siblings. I do not need to dress as something else for Halloween. I am already a ghost.* It is why, often, I've thought it would not matter if I were no longer alive. I am not real, anyway. Not a being like everyone else, being here. Who would miss me since I don't exist to begin with?

Psychoanalyst Donald Woods Winnicott made famous the idea of "continuity of being." He claimed that if a child experiences "a good enough mother," one who meets their physical, emotional, and psychological need for safety and care; one who reflects back to the child a true sense of reality, then the child develops "a true self."

Simply put, they can be exactly who they are with the mother, can grow and adapt to the coming slow and repetitious change that occurs along with the mother, and that she will, as the baby grows into child, teenager, young adult, always accept them.

The alternative is a disreality: "experiences of existential continuity," wrote Winnicott, a rupture in the continuity of self. A false self is created to project to the mother, the only self safe enough to be made available to her. The child, Winnicott claims, turns reality into something that can be intellectualized, but without emotions, affections, or (most curious to me) creative acts.

I may not be real, but the creative act is. It is like clouds, abstract but present. Intangible, but look! my hands are moving, touching something. But what? What, in my life, have I moved toward every day but constantly and consistently toward language? I hold it up in front of me, daily, as if it could save my life. I play with it and in playing with it, become more real.

Who can see me?

DEVASTATION

The mind tries to both wall and unwall the self. This I know. I've understood its method as a means to interpret the world, while simultaneously protecting from the violence and chaos that comes with that interpretation. There is little that can be done if one wishes to live accurately and wholly. Pain, eventually, gets in.

Hence, devastation.

The first time I knew devastation, it was not my own. But I understood it, even at age eleven, as a kind of obliteration of the present. A man had gone into an elementary school in Scotland and killed 16 children. What was there would never be there again. In my child-mind, it was incomprehensible. But I remember days later, on a chilly March morning, filling my mittens with rocks in the schoolyard. *I will hold these in front of me*, I thought, *if a bullet comes flying.* I did comprehend, even then, that the world can take everything away from you.

Devastation derives from the past participle stem of the Latin *devastare*: *de-* meaning "completely," *vastare* meaning "lay waste," "empty," "desolate." When someone says, "that is devastating" what they feel is that suffering has been put into motion. I have my own definitions of suffering:

> "plunged,"
> "going dark,"
> "constant delay,"
> "an endless reproduction,"
> "a slaughterhouse,"
> "wearing burning clothes in a burning world,"
> "everything, because, nothing."

Roland Barthes defined suffering as "the impossibility of being comfortable anywhere." He wrote this in his mourning diary, after the death of his mother. I imagine him shifting in his chair as he wrote it. The chair transformed, now just a stiff object, a hard shape, to which his body would no longer conform. *Chair* no longer a chair.

My mother is still living, though she is gone from me. A different kind of death, where possibility could exist. But instead, it looks like this:

Old Latin: *Extraneus* (not belonging)   →   Medieval Latin: *Extraneare* (treated as a stranger)   →   French: *Estranger* (a stranger)   → Modern English: *Estranged* (what I am)

I am the adjective, as it is happening, in perpetuity. Is it easier, knowing she is alive, that she walks around breathing, her body somewhere on the earth and not in it; in a house, being, where I will never again be?

I also cannot find a chair I can sit in.

On November 4, 1977, Barthes wrote: "Around 6 p.m.: the apartment is warm, clean, well-lit, pleasant. I make it that way, energetically, devotedly (enjoying it bitterly): henceforth and forever I am my own mother." He has this realization nine days after his mother dies. He is sixty-two years old.

This provokes a memory for me:

> *When I was ten, our bunnies had babies and had babies. The mother bunny rejected them, pushed the babies out of the cage, and so my mother took them inside, fed them with an eye dropper and tried to keep them alive. But they all died. They needed their mother.*

That "she desired to mother others," is a sentence that makes itself dark to me. I feel now, as Barthes still felt at sixty-two, this kind of devastation.

Henceforth, I am, forever now, my own mother.

His ability to see the value in suffering is what draws me to him most, as he explains, "My suffering is inexpressible but at the same time utterable, speakable. The very fact that language affords me the word 'intolerable' immediately achieves a certain tolerance."

How do I tolerate my suffering? Is this what I have to learn to do? To carry it with me in my arms like my own cradled child, tend to it like a farmer's last viable crop? Can I attain tolerance by knowing I am in the same company as Barthes? That he is like kin to me? That, in some way, we have suffered in the same way?

One day, late in the first year of his mourning, he wrote in succession: "I live in my suffering and that makes me happy."

Then, "Anything that keeps me from my suffering is unbearable."

And later that same day, "I ask for nothing but to lie in my suffering."

His suffering became a necessity, a possessive noun: thing that belonged to him just as his own mind, carried with him like a second consciousness. Barthes called it "enormous," and said, "the high seas of suffering—leaves the shores, nothing in sight." This feeling of isolation is prevalent in his text and the writing happened only in little bursts the year after his mother's death. Barthes kept this diary, writing down thoughts and discoveries, rarely more than a page; a small collection of words to collect his grief. Bewilderment at what's sayable about the unsayable.

I see it now, from where I am. Devastation is when there is no going back.

NONFICTION

Que sais-je?

In a dream once, I traveled toward my mother on the back of a red-brown horse, through towns and cityscapes and heavy night and gray fog and merciless winds. Geography was endless, though it signaled, through passage and movement and the world of blurring shapes, that space could be navigated, collapsed down. Like my mother, the horse, too, didn't want me and so hurled me around so that I was inches from her backbone at every other moment. I was, in effect, thrown up and down in simultaneity, into the half-lit and darkening sky. From a distance, the outline of my mother stood against a bright and angry sea. She could be measured against the horizon. But no matter how fast the horse galloped, how much land we covered, I never got closer to her, (though she remained, always, in my eye-gaze). She was both absence and presence, longing and distance, reachable and unreachable. The harder I snapped the reins, the more the horse threw me violently from side to side. I thought of abandoning the horse and running across the earth to her, but when I looked down my feet had disintegrated away; nothing there but two stubs rawed at their ends. I cried an animal cry, but there was no one to hear me. And if the mother could, had ears and opened them, the sea might drown out my sound so that I was mistaken for a wave's crashing. Or another child crying. I thought, *I am alone in the world.* I thought, *the mother is there, I just can't get to her.*

Love, as you know, is a difficult subject.

Even in the dream, I could not fathom the impossible idea that no matter how long it took, I would never reach her. Even when my hands began to disintegrate, too, and I could no longer hold on to the reins or the horse's mane. Even when the horse disappeared, and I was a floating subject, bouncing across space through endless time. Even when the world became so dark, I could no longer see what was in front of me: the mother, the horizon, the sea. Even when I stopped thinking and closed my eyes and slept, dreaming in the dream. Even then, I could not understand it.

I am rattling now, as in the dream, through the physics of memory, across experimental surfaces. What story do I want to tell and how do I tell it?

14

I entered this not knowing what language could do for me. Knowing only that it would not stop doing it.

"The continuous work of our life is to build death," wrote Michel de Montaigne. But rather, I think it is to defy erasure in the inevitable building of death.

What do I know? That as long as I write, I cannot be erased.

Memory has worked to bring me here. Everything that was once unimaginable to me I manage now only though imagination. How do I distinguish what is verifiable from what is unverifiable? How do I tell the truth of a fact that only my mind owns? Sometimes I do not know how to compare what is remembered, what is imagined, the way the wind changes in me, the conditions that pain creates, or how to follow the direction of my two minds that scurry along as opposite swimming fish. But I do have this one wish: to not be disappeared to the world as I have been to the mother.

Like Montaigne wrote, "my ideas and my judgment merely grope their way forward, faltering, tripping, and stumbling." Progression is the ultimate illusion. That we can arrive somewhere different than where we began. But still we try, as if movement were a promise the legs make to the body, the mind to its pain.

Try. Even if you remain in fragment, like pieces of jade dropped from a storm's mouth and strewn all over a childhood beach you remember the feeling of, but whose name you have forgotten.

Or does the infinitive mean one is in a constant state of motion, suspended in action as if held there without regard to time; no suffix to push the action into the past tense?

[To be disoriented.]

To look at old photographs.

To wonder if every mother is yours.

To negotiate the past.

To think an image is fact.

To match your hair color to a nameless wildflower.

To drink bourbon from a glass.

To call yourself a rendering.

To remember in rendered episodes.

To go outside as the day turns into night.

To try and witness change.

NARRATION

I want to tell a story that defies story-logic.

A story against Aristotle and his "whole"; his beginning, middle, and end; his perfect split of action: complication, then unravelling.

The story of a trauma lacks wholeness. It is an event without a direct witness. "A narrative of belated experience," scholar Cathy Caruth calls it, describing it as a "breach in the mind's experience of time, self, and the world . . . not available to consciousness until it imposes itself again, repeatedly . . ."

Once I was a daughter, then I wasn't. This is one way of telling the story.

Once I was run out of my childhood home, no longer a child, but still—hers. I slept on the airport floor too stunned to think. This is another way of telling it.

Once I was born, small helpless thing to the wrong mother. I'm sure I was held, feed, clothed, bathed, even kissed. But I do not remember this.

When a therapist asked me in our first meeting if I still loved my mother, I said yes quickly as if I could erase the question by answering it.

Once I walked a rural path in Italy, winced in the afternoon light and dropped to my knees under a quince tree and wept.

The whole story is order-less. How do I re-witness it?

Every moment of remembering is an injurious repetition. Caruth wrote, "The return of the traumatic experience in the dream is not the signal of the direct experience but, rather, of the attempt to overcome the fact that it was not direct, to attempt to master what was never fully grasped in the first place."

I know the dilemma is not in the remembering, but in the grasping.

I lost the mother twice. First, in the initial losing, the geographical separation. Her desire to remove me from the family system. The second, when I realized I was as good as dead to her. That she had other children to fulfill her needs. That I was disposable, could be easily erased.

But repeatedly I've dreamt she welcomed me back to the family, begged even, only for me to die shortly after. One might think this ironic, but perhaps it is the pinnacle of necessity: to have a desire I don't desire, fulfilled.

I don't want her back. At least, that's what I tell myself now. I wonder how many repetitions it takes for an idea to become a truth. How much the action of repeating is at odds with the action of progress? Repetition until the story becomes endless, without distinguishable form?

What if there is no resolution to my loss? No beginning, middle, and end. Does a story need one? Is any form possible when it comes to the disordered and unstable activity of writing trauma?

I dream of the end, but never reach one. Thus, it does not exist. This thought is enough to make me stop. But for some reason, I can't. My mind pulls me forward like a horse pulling its carriage.

"Freud made the distinction between the rules that govern conscious life and the unconscious realm of dreams," writes narratologist Kent Puckett, "The conscious mind organizes, regulates, and binds thought in terms of certain temporal and causal rules."

He states that, according to Freud, two things cannot occupy the same point in time or space in the conscious mind, though in the unconscious, "ideas can be stacked allusively or metaphorically or interchangeably on top of each other."

This is the challenge I now face: how to get my two minds to sync together like two lungs working, simultaneously, toward breath.

How to live and keep living.

So I go back to the beginning and begin again:

Once I was her daughter.

Then I wasn't.

The end.

TRANSLATION

1.

Why, in a house, is there a room named for "living" but not for "loving"?

Perhaps the mother should answer. She was so specific in her giving. Built a house and filled it up with children. Gave life easily, but not love. Said, *now, go and try to live.* Outsourced her pain to the children who lassoed it up, carried it across each other (where?) across each other (where?), etymologically, all the way across.

2.

In my world, the word *mother* translates to *stranger.* Don't ask me why. I learned it in the brute form of language, English to English, in some early dark-light of childhood.

Now I have a word, I thought. Which also means, *now I've lost a word.*

3.

Let me paraphrase (loanwords are needed): always *Quid Pro Quo*, my *Mea Culpa*, to the *Hoi Polloi.* Perhaps her *Schadenfreude* is *Le Mot Juste.* In other words, she hauled us like a horse, washed our nested hair, sang "see I cared for you so well" while stirring the dinner sauce. Distinction never fell away. The word *child* remained *child* (for appearances). But the children themselves became *golden, goat,* or *lost.*

4.

I know you want narrative. I'm trying. A family is a small population with its own language. And for those on the outside, all I can give is a rendering: *mother, father, child, child, child, child, child, child, child, child.* I must have been unastonishing among them. Let's call this, as Francis Bacon says, *the brutality of fact.*

5.

Memory purchases the abstract. There are flashpoints, fractions, a
hinterland of hurt. No boundaries but a brink. No codes but a lifetime of
decoding. A dimming switch on each child and *thou shalt not feel* written
nowhere (but readable). I learned things through neglect, not command, in
unspoken language: *you, child, should be not heard and not seen.* Which now
I realize reads:

You are bad because you tried to say exactly what you mean.

6.

I tried to write *the darknesses inside me are violent,* but instead wrote *violet.* Is
error, too, a form of translation? Is it an error to suggest it as so?

The violet in me wants to know.

7.

I was taught metaphrase as a formal equivalence. Exact words becoming
exact words. It's taken me many to reach this: the family is untranslatable,
my *mise-en-abyme.* Which translates directly to *placed into an abyss.*

8.

The house is either a pulse or a plot. The mother decides it. The house
can't be translated away. It's still there in its blue-beige, its white door and
is missed, mostly, at noon. But if you walk around carefully (even in the
mind) you'll find there is a wound in every room.

9.

I read a translation of the Émile Nelligan line, "Do you want me to astralize
the night?" It's taken me days to decipher:

Do you want me to star the night?

Do you want me to make 'of night' the starlight of night?

Or more simply,

Do you want some light in your night?

I live in its difficulty. Maybe some darkness is central to meaning. Or maybe darkness is meaning.

10.

In the house, there was no room for loving.

SELECTION

So many theories, of which theories become truth. And Darwin with his superior and inferior. His advantaged and disadvantaged. *Fair game,* he might have said. *Compete, it is natural.* It is natural to have a functional advantage, to live and die by that sudden, advantageous leap.

*

"I'm a fair mother," the mother might have said, as she plated one child in gold. While another, with goat-eyes, watched on.

*

Scapegoat: a noun from Leviticus 16, the archaic *scape* meaning *escape* + *goat:* bearer of sins; goat that is sent away, punished for the mistakes of others, into the wild alone, carrying through the desert all that weight.

*

Within dysfunctional families, it is common for the strongest-minded child to be chosen. An assigned role, a subconscious fate. The role is designed to hold you down, so that you cannot reveal the mother's games.

*

The verb *to scapegoat* is an ego-defense, according to psychoanalytic theory. It means to project onto another one's own destructive innards.

*

"The life of the scapegoat (noun) is tragic," one article says. *Tragedy,* from the Greek word *tragoidia,* meaning *goat-song.* Now the crescendo of one rises.

TRAUMATIZATION

Blue slate of the sky laid itself out for us. My husband and I drove down the California coast, as if driving were an act of erasing. When we rounded the rail-less curves in Big Sur, I screamed and gripped the seat. I talked with my eyes closed, past the most fathomly beautiful scene.

Though I grew up swimming in the Atlantic, the Pacific did not completely stun me. When I opened the window, the ocean was every ocean I had ever put myself in. I was a child again briefly; salt hit my lungs. Even with the country stretched long between her and me, and the time and years that had brought me here, it was only in this moment that I began to understand that I've been traumatized by my mother.

Trauma: the Greek word for *wound*. A word I'd never thought, in this context, I'd have to use.

Birth wound.
Time wound.
Light wound.
New wound.
Old wound.
The sound-of-her-voice wound.
Trust wound.
Dark wound.
Thought wound.
Thinking wound.
Lover wound.
Mother wound.

It is sometimes called an affliction, I learn.

*

Five years together in New York, then five in California. Marriage is a phenomenological thing. We didn't love each other less, but the loving was more glassy. I feared at any moment we would break. Who was the one less loved, was not a question I needed answered. There were many nights I had to beg him to turn his body around. To be toward me. I wanted to not be ignored by him, as I was by the mother.

*

A *mother wound* becomes a *lover wound*
and then you have double wounds.
A deeper affliction. I learned this late,
at the end of marriage.

*

Campgrounds are for lovers. We drove past them, until the sun began to dip below San Simeon. Each night I thought, this will be the night he will make his way past the darkness to my body. An empty motel by the Pacific has the ability to be momentous. But he'd fall asleep immediately. Hoops the size and shape of different wounds fell, in sequences, down through me. I have been, my whole life, designed by them.

Now I understand this: what the nervous system remembers is what is remembered. The body knows what the mind cannot. No action can stop it. When I hear a child in the supermarket scream uncontrollably for her mother, my body shakes and cannot stop.

*

I hope by writing this language can jar a wound.

I wish this is what I knew: a new life in California does not mean love is renewed. My husband never noticed what I was reading, but every night when I curled away from him, I entered theories.

The more I read, the more I learned that traumatic memories lack narrative and context. They are encoded in the form of image and sensation and also called *indelible* or *death images*. Psychologist Pierre Janet explained this: "Like all psychological phenomena, memory is an action, it is the action of telling a story... a situation has not been satisfactorily liquidated until we achieve, not merely an outward reaction through our movements, but also an inward reaction through the words we address to ourselves."

It was Freud who called the recurrent intrusion of traumatic experience the "repetition compulsion." An idée fixe. It comes and it comes as if the sea and you must enter it, even if you can't remember exactly how. Trauma shatters the inner schemata of the brain. Psychiatrist Abram Kardiner describes this

26

experience, writing: "the whole apparatus for concerted, coordinated and purposeful activity is smashed."

I think it is still true that if you stay on the road and keep moving, you are circumnavigating it. The pain. Keep the wheels turning and try to reinvent the broken-down schema of the brain.

DYSFUNCTION

During my first winter in Ohio, I sat with the great poet in a hotel lobby. She was visiting the university and had come to talk about my poems.

"You know," she said, before any formal introduction, "the greatest myth ever told is that all mothers can love their children." She said, "can love," as if no fault should be bestowed. As if it is an abnormality claimed by some force that is out-of-the-mother's-hands.

She held my poems in front of her, seconds passed and then I heard, "What I understand from this is bad, bad . . . not a good mother."

I waited for more, but there was silence.

She said she was sorry, that she couldn't help me with that, but that there was something she could tell me.

She asked me if I knew how "living rooms" got their names. Before I could answer, she explained.

Up until the late nineteenth century, these rooms were called parlours, she said. A word that derives from the old French word "parloir" or "parler" which means "to speak." Gatherings happened in them. Sometimes happy events, like weddings or births, but most often the dead were laid out here before funeral parlors came into existence. People would gather between these walls at the side of beloveds to say their mournful goodbyes.

So, she said, laughing, "The 'living room' is actually the 'death room' . . . ironic huh?"

In an essay, once, the great poet wrote, "The human mind is capable of a great elastic theater."

And surely, this is it. This thought-game we play. The meaning of words detached from their meaning. This spectatorship of our own thinking.

In another piece, "A Short Lecture on Translation," which I read after our meeting, she discusses a translator friend who offers an historical example of the first known translation in mankind. In this piece, the great poet decides the translator's answer is wrong. She writes instead, "surely it was when a mother heard her baby babble and cry, and had to decide in an instant what it meant."

(When I read this back to myself months later, alone in my living room, the mid-January day dark as evening, I let out an audible sound. Not quite a wail or a whimper, but something animal, low. With no one around to hear it, I look down at my arms and see my mother's arms: brown freckles dotted all over from the sun. My arm indistinguishable from the image I held of hers. My arm on fire, burning, even though it is winter.)

After we finished discussing death rooms, the great poet asked me if I wanted a cigarette. I said I did not.

So we continued to sit together, and we didn't make another sound.

Outside the Ohio snow fell up and down.

CONJUGATION

Just as language moves us, we must move language. It is our human job:

to be, to go, to see, to love in, to run on, to lose, to die

It's not so hard. Verbs imply action. Action implies movement. Movement implies we are alive (at least in the moment of moving). So, language, too, must be alive. For a long time, I've considered myself a mover of language. I've found myself in the most difficult of rooms, furnished with big pieces that house and comfort and stand in ornate fashion. This is all true. But the furniture is words, and I shift and arrange them to stand in their sometimes rightful, sometimes wrongful places.

I don't know how I became this way, but I've always fervently desired possibility. And verbs, in all their forms, provide it:

irregular
present
past
perfective
continuous
active
passive
linked
delexical
modal
reflexive
infinitive

The possibilities keep me moving.

The verb signals an action, an occurrence, or a state of being. Whether mental, physical, or mechanical, verbs always express activity. "The verb," C.D. Wright wrote, "works the hardest, so it should be the best paid."

The first time I remember conjugating verbs, I did so in French. I did so trying to understand the possibilities of knowing (I was twelve, what could I know?):

je sais

tu sais

il sait

nous savons

vous savez

ils savent

Conjugation, by definition, is "the creation of derived forms of a verb from its principal parts by inflection." It may be affected by person, number, gender, tense, aspect, mood, or voice. It involves roots and stems, patterns and rules:

je sais

je saurai

je savais

je sache

je saurais

je susse

What I know and don't know is full of possibility. Any rule can be learned and then unlearned.

It's taken me thirty years to understand the rules of my mother. Mostly unspoken. Mostly unfollowable: Be my mirror, don't be my mirror. You are not wanted here, but you are not to leave. Verb contradictions. It's why I so desire to understand *mother* as a verb.

> mother: *to bestow a maternal action upon*
> mothered: *to have once had this action, so, no longer*
> mothering: *happening constantly, in the present, so, very lucky*
> mutter: *how I sound when I speak, how I try not to sound*
> moth: *batted away, thing unwanted*
> muster: *all I could, can*
> mud: *as good as*

I break every rule by simply being, according to the mother.

was, went, saw, loved, ran, lost, died

When applied directly back to her, only the past tense is warranted. I had a mother once. Once I had a mother. "Had" shows possession, which isn't exactly correct. A mother was there. But she was never mine.

I remember wanting her badly, clinging to her like a fish, grasping her, holding her, touching her hand, gripping her back, smelling her hair, kissing her head. Every action repeated. Every repetition desperate with active love.

Action verbs denote the present.

It was just last night I did this. I clung to her in a dream. Like no time, like no time.

What tense describes *never again*? If the spatial differences of time are measured by conjugations, then what inflection denotes complete absence? When I ask language, language tells me to keep moving:

mother, mama, ma mère, merely

APPELLATION

I was named by my mother. Most are. And by this naming, was said into existence.

Your name is the sound that scaffolds the shape of you.

Historically, in some parts of the Congo, mothers refused to name their babies until the measles had passed. It was too painful, I read, for the child to be thought of as lasting.

But I did last. Born early, premature, rocked apart by the natural pains of the world. My name just another ancient convention. I feel as though from it I am disappearing. Why? Because she no longer says it. I wonder what happens when one is erased by their mother? Who can tell me, outside of her, that I still exist? And if I stop saying the word *mother*, will she?

*

> Of vulnerability, I said the pronoun. That is the answer,
> to remove her name as dark is removed from a light night.
> A substitute for the noun, a word now illogical in its form:
> why say *mother* when I can just say *her*? A demotion
> down. Now that she's not even a noun I can place her
> syntactically elsewhere. Call her Foucault's "unthought."
> Is a poem just a little sculpture of words? A way of
> understanding all that I now see? Built much like the thought:
> *Are all mothers broken? No, just broken is she.* Logic works best
> when it cannot be found, when it's revealed in a series
> of tests we once knew, like the sequence: *her, her her.* Like
> a song a different mother might have sung, in a different life.
> But now I owe my thinking to the one thing I've been taught:
> language has been gentle with me the way people have not.

*

When I was little, she sometimes called me *Kimmerie*. Left out the harshest syllables. The *barely*.

It is not so often that I am left without language. But when I am and when there is nothing left to say, or way to say it, it is like a flock of birds across my throat, like a flock between myself and that "to" that marks all action; all that is inexpressible and the sometimes always murmurmative expression of it.

[To say nothing, do nothing, mark time, to bend,
to straighten up, to blame oneself,]

to go outside of the self in that blaming.

To look for a fist in every hand.

To walk across a city a hundred times.

To resist the ocean and turn toward the trees.

To see history as one possible memory.

To imagine the home that swells in you.

To not understand differences of place.

To hold your head to the sky's blue socket.

To think every juxtaposition is a waste.

JUXTAPOSITION

One crisis hides another crisis. It is not unlike the way two trains next to each other conceal and reveal their rectangles when moving back and forth. The mind is the conductor of feeling.

*

I am on a train moving toward Manhattan. It is in the absence of my husband that he emerges fully. Twelve years, two coasts, and eventually Ohio breaks us. I've ridden this train before, past the dilapidated buildings colored in graffiti, through Queens, our route toward the first city I loved him in. The city has stayed, so has the love, but now he is gone. Here begins the film strip of our every past movement. Here begins the problem of proximity. I try to gather everything our marriage was made of in my head and place each thing next to each other to create a narrative. But nothing coherent comes. On the train, I open *A Lover's Discourse*, can't read past the table of contents, Barthes' own (and then my) image-repertoire:

to be engulfed,

absence, adorable, affirmation, alteration,
anxiety, annulment,

askesis, *atopos*,

waiting,
to hide,
pigeonholed,

catastrophe,

to circumscribe, heart, fulfillment, compassion,

to understand, behavior,

connivance, contacts, contingencies,

body,

declaration, dedication, demons, dependency,

expenditure, disreality, drama,

flayed, to write, errantry,

embrace, exile,

irksome,

fade-out, faults, festivity,

mad, embarrassment,

Gradiva, habiliment, identification,

image, unknowable,

induction, informer, unbearable

outcomes, jealousy, i-love-you, languor, letter, *loquela*, magic, monstrous,
silence, clouds, night, objects, obscene, crying, gossip,

why, ravishment,

regretted, encounter, reverberation,

waking, scene, alone,

signs, remembrance, suicide, thus,
tenderness, union, truth,

will-to-possess.

*

I place MOTHER next to LOVER

LOVER next to MOTHER

To see how neither could love me

outside of their own dysfunctions

*

One crisis reveals another crisis. One time, in the presence of no one but ourselves, the husband and I rode the train up the peninsula to San Francisco, dressed in our wedding clothes, and married each other behind a large Christmas tree decorated with paper cranes in a government building. From this memory: daubs of neck light and his face soaked and hovering above mine. From this memory, I gather the time that has spooled itself on the floor.

From love, I want to remove the howling. Excise it like a spleen. I want to believe that this howling is not a necessity. Barthes wrote that there's "nothing more lacerating than a voice at once beloved and exhausted." He defined fatigue as infinity: "what never manages to end." Perhaps this is the part of losing that is required. That with or without the howling, all absence would still burn a hole in me. Like that time I asked my husband for a match in four feet of snow to demonstrate how a circle burns itself so round, you can see straight through to the ground. *This is what you do to me*, I had told him. The metaphor ignored. My language never suited him. Another image to demonstrate the way we contrasted each other: my presence burning into his absence. Two trains moving past each other infinitely.

And infinitely, without end, forever and ever now, I have no mother.

CURATION

Light operates the walls. The room exists in shadow-shapes. I imagine, as a child, newly born, I looked up and thought everything in my eye-view would be mine forever. A misunderstanding of place. But a little life that makes it all the way out of the mother should have such expectations.

When a child is born, the mother is not yet perceived as mother.

She is God and the world.

She is weather, pleasure, and time.

She lights the room or darkens it. Creates form. Each new day.

Every answer to when, where, how and why.

The mother tends to the child, bends the child, fends for the child; breaks the child, and wakes the child, sometimes bakes cakes for the child. These gestures make the child.

Like:

Holds child's cracker. So child holds cracker. Hugs child and so child hugs back. Smiles or doesn't smile. Child thinks she's good, thinks she's bad, is sad, combative, glad. Mother teaches the child to sit, crawl, walk, roll, brush hair, and teeth; shirt and pants go this way, fork to mouth, the ABC's; the sound of language, loud sounds, softer, forgetting and finding; what fire is, water, sin, how to swim and how to pump your legs on a swing; what will hurt, what will sting; shoes, their ties, songs, how to sing them; what anger is, and yelling, and hate; what is owed back, and what all this is; how to see and how to witness.

Then, she demonstrates the swervings of love and not-love, each, but not their difference.

The mother assembles, maintains, manages the child's growing. She trains the child to think dysfunction is function. Wrong is right. Only some people are allowed to have a voice and to fight.

If light tenderizes the walls, then light erases the walls.

The mother has first access to the child-mind. A careful tilling. She builds the child before the child builds a self. She creates the whole.

Anything that comes after is a process of undoing.

Curator, from the Middle English *curat*: person charged with the care of a soul.

REPRESENTATION

One summer, while house-sitting a large home in California, I stare at a painting every day. It hangs in the kitchen where I stir and then dispose of my coffee spoon in a fancy farm-style sink. The house belongs to a psychiatrist who is in Vienna for the summer. He has given me the space to write and in return, I water his flowers, retrieve the mail. The painting, by René Magritte, is of an apple, its brilliant red fading to green, with a French phrase scribbled above it:

Ceci n'est pas une pomme.

This is not an apple.

Strange, I think, the first time I see it. But then again, Magritte was interested in playing with logic, in making the ordinary unusual. Among his most famous paintings was a portrait called *Les Amants*, which depicted lovers obscuring their faces with cloth.

His constant play with reality and illusion has been attributed to the early death of his mother. When Magritte was thirteen years old, she committed suicide, after many previous attempts, by drowning herself in the River Sambre. According to witnesses, he was present when her body was recovered from the water and it had been reported that, when found, her dress was covering her face.

Magritte described his paintings as "visible images which conceal nothing; they evoke mystery and, indeed, when one sees one of my pictures, one asks oneself this simple question, 'What does that mean?'. It does not mean anything, because mystery means nothing either, it is unknowable."

His play with reality and illusion is a formal mirror held to the experience of his traumatic loss. If "what is" can be claimed to be "not," then perhaps (illogically) his mother's death can be undone. This activity permeates his work, whereas the essence of an object can only ever be created as a new representation, never (like the permanence of death) actually recovered.

In another painting, Magritte famously repeats a similar logic: "Ceci n'est pas une pipe," he wrote over a picture of a pipe. Later, he offered further examination:

The famous pipe. How people reproached me for it! And yet, could you stuff my pipe? No, it's just a representation, is it not? So if I had written on my picture 'This is a pipe,' I'd have been lying!

What he means is: the word is not the thing, as the map is not the place. The way the mother, in this story, is not my mother. Not exactly.

Ceci n'est pas une pomme.
Ceci n'est pas une pipe.
Ceci n'est pas une bouche.
Ceci n'est pas une bleue.
Ceci n'est pas un arbre.
Ceci n'est pas une fleur.
Ceci n'est pas une maison.
Ceci n'est pas une ville.
Ceci n'est pas un pays.
Ceci n'est pas une langue.
Ceci n'est pas un monde.
Ceci n'est pas un carte du monde.
Ceci n'est pas un son.
Ceci n'est pas une chanson.
Ceci n'est pas une ancienne chanson.
Ceci n'est pas l'art.
Ceci n'est pas une image de.
Ceci n'est pas une image.
Ceci n'est pas une personne.
Ceci n'est pas ton esprit.
Ceci n'est pas la mer.
Ceci n'est pas la mère.
Ceci n'est pas nouvelle langue.
Ceci n'est pas un doigt pointé.
Ceci n'est pas une pensée.
Ceci n'est pas un poème.

"How can one learn the truth by thinking? As one learns to see a face better if one draws it," wrote Wittgenstein.

When language eludes me, I turn to schemes: figures to denote the shape of something I cannot otherwise form. *Scheme* from the Latin *schema* and Greek *skhema*, meaning "figure I hold."

The physiological trauma story:

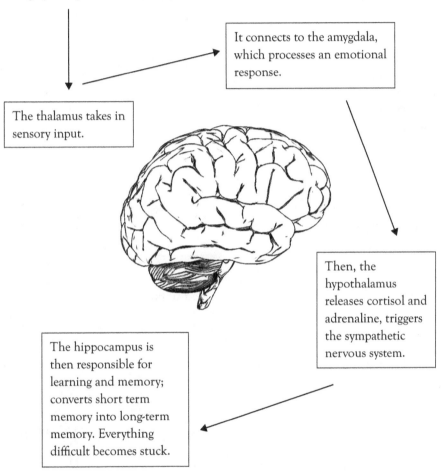

It connects to the amygdala, which processes an emotional response.

The thalamus takes in sensory input.

Then, the hypothalamus releases cortisol and adrenaline, triggers the sympathetic nervous system.

The hippocampus is then responsible for learning and memory; converts short term memory into long-term memory. Everything difficult becomes stuck.

When I think of my brain I do not think of intellect or knowledge. I think of broken synapses, a shrunken hippocampus, a sphere of memory and pain so strong, it keeps me from myself. I think of endings, of Dickinson, *a funeral in my brain, Wrecked, solitary, here.* But also, *there.*

DISSOCIATION

Fort! Da! Fort! Da! Fort! Da! Fort! Da! Fort! Da! Fort! Da! Fort! Da! Fort! Da!
Fort! Da! Fort! Da! Fort! Da! Fort! Da! Fort! Da! Fort! Da! Fort! Da! Fort! Da!
Fort! Da! Fort! Da! Fort! Da! Fort! Da! Fort! Da! Fort! Da! Fort! Da!
Fort! Da! Fort! Da! Fort! Da! Fort! Da! Fort! Da! Fort! Da! Fort! Da! Fo   Da!
Fo ! Da! Fort! Da! Fort! Da! Fort! Da! Fort! [   ] Da! Fort! Da! F
Fort   ! Fort! Da! Fort! Da! Fort! Da! Fort! Da! Fort! Da! Fort! Da!
Fort!   Da! Fort!   rt! Da! Fort! Da! Fort! Da!
Fort! L   a! Fort! Da!
Fort! Da   ! Fort! Da! Fort! Da! Fort!
Fort! Da!   Da. Fort! Da! F
Fort! Da! Fo.   ! D   Da
Fort! Da! Fort.
Fort! Da! Fort! L   Da.
Fort! Da! Fo ! Da.   a! Fort! Da!
Fort! Da! F   Da! Fort! Da.
Fort!   Fort! Da! Fort   ort! Da!
Fort! Da! Fort! Da! Fort!   Da!   Da!
Fort! Da! Fort! Da! Fort! Da!   a! Fort! Da! Fort! Da!
  rt! Da! Fort! Da! Fort! Da!   Da!   a! Fo   Da!
Fort! Da! Fort! Da!   c   Da! Fort! Da! Fort! Da!
F   a   ort! Da! Fort!
                        Da! Fort   Fort! Da! Fort! Da!
                      d! Da! Fort! a! Fo   Fort! Da!
                 ort! D   d! Da! Fort! Da   Da!
              . F   ort! Da! Fort! Da! Fort! Da! Fort! Da!
               Da'   Fort! Da! Fort! Da! Fort! Da! Fort! Da!
                   ! D   a!
   Fort! Da! Fort! D   ort! Da! Fort! Da! Fort! Da! Fort! Da.
Fort! Da! F   Fort! Da! Fort! Da! Fort! Da! Fort! Da! F   Da!
F   Da! Fort! Da! Fort! Da! Fort! Da! Fort! Da! Fort! Da! Fort! Da! F   a!
Fort! Da.   Da!   Da! Fort! Da! Fort! Da! Fo   Da!
  ort! Da! Fort! Da! Fort! Da! Fort! Da! Fort! Da! Fort! Da! Fort! Da! Fort! Da!
Fort! F Fort! Da! Fort! Da! Fort! Da! Fort! Da! Fort! Da! Fort! Da! Fort! Da!
    a! Fort! Da! Fort! Da! Fort! Da! Fort! Da! Fort! Da! Fort! Da! Fort! Da!
    Da! Fort! Da! Fort! Da! Fort! Da! Fort! Da! Fort! Da! Fort! Da!
  rt! Da! Fort! Da! Fort! Da! Fort! Da! Fort! Da! Fort! Da! Fort! Da! Fort! Da!
Fort! Da! Fort! Da.   Da!

INTERPRETATION

Trauma is of the body. But first, it starts in the brain:

1. *Thinking Center*

to

2. *Emotion Center*

to

3. *Fear Center*

One section is underactive (thinking) and two are overactive (emotion and fear). An article calls the brain in a trauma state "bottom-heavy," meaning the lower, more primal areas of the brain are in overload.

When I was at the height of my trauma, my mind could not rest or reset. I was hypervigilant at all times, living in an extended awareness, ready to attack anything that might hurt me. I would lie awake at night, almost levitating, ready to jump at the initial phoneme of any sound.

I could not, no matter how I tried, see the world and people around me as anything but a threat.

But the most fundamental frustration of trauma for me has not been its experience, but its explanation. I research charts and send them to others, explain the physiology of it, the psychology, the biology, the ways my brain has been changed. But still, people don't always believe me. They want to make their own interpretation of the trauma. Write the story of it themselves.

*

A student once asked me if I became a writer to interpret my own life. Of course not, I said. I became a writer to make things.

But what am I making? Is this not an attempt at interpretation? A desire to understand an event in my life so traumatizing, I must constantly escape reality into the mechanisms of language?

"The earliest theory of art," wrote Susan Sontag, "proposed that art was mimesis, imitation of reality." I am reading her essay "Against Interpretation," trying to interpret it. An explication of meaning.

Sontag claims that it is this theory of mimesis that challenges art to justify itself. Explain its own existence. This is what I am also doing. Trying to justify myself, my here-ness.

"Even a painting of a bed would be only an 'imitation of an imitation,'" she says, quoting Plato, the philosopher who disliked poets, thought they were merely image-makers, reproducers of the world, incapable of truth; all poets exiled in *The Republic*, left outside the walls of the ideal city.

I am an exile too, I think. But this is also not completely true. My exile is familial, a form of banishment I can't find in any article or book. Not political or religious or geographical. There are no definitions for what has happened to me. I've taken to calling it erasure, imagining the small traces of my life still present to my mother, even in my absence, just scratched out.

There is no way to really know, though. I am not an origin text. I have not been written down. Am not, no matter how hard I try, explicable.

I have found that there is no finding, only the propensity to find, which is, in its own inconclusive way, a forever task.

[To find tenderness in stones.]

To concentrate on the contractions of a bird's rib.

To believe in the pain of all things.

To think a gorge is a strange place for water.

To love regardless.

To travel the distances required to make one a traveler.

To hold a face in the space of your arms.

To form thought into a cathedral of thinking.

To study the architecture of sun.

INTELLECTUALIZATION

It is through an aspect of mind we interpret
the proper scaffolding

in which to fasten memory

I was little once and the smallness of me did
not warrant attention, as a child among
several, all needing, I was

(a conflict)

lost on a beach one day, near mother, in sight, the sun
hot and my five-year old body forgotten for hours

wherein pain is a collaboration between
the body and the mind

(a glittering continuous-ness)

and years later, while mindless with desire, a lover's body
affixed to my backside like a button, there was
the illusion of fire

I find translation electric

Anna Freud might say "purposeful"

wherein I said to the lover as he showered me,
do you think she heard me in the night
when I cried?

(a transition to reason)

go to sleep, I was told

how I remember my back's whole world
blistering, red suns bleeding

through my nightshirt

(a defense)

there's always a secret scaffolding
to hold language

to which the lover said, *you know language
might not always accept such action*

(I can't remember
how to properly remember)

that lover has gone now, moved
to Mazatlán

what do you do with a backbone
you can't love?

fashioning a response is always
an achievement of

the mind
(which mothers me)

reports the imagination:

you let the sun burn it.

RECONJUGATION

Because language is never one thing, if you change the inflection of the syllable in the word *conjugate*, you get the algebraic word *conjugate*: when the sign in the middle of two terms is changed to its opposite:

$$X + Y \text{ becomes } X - Y$$

(child + mother becomes child − mother)

This is described as a "rationale"

I do research and a website tells me a conjugate is the binomial formed by the negative of the second term of the binomial. It says X *and* Y *are real numbers, though if* Y *is imaginary then the process is termed "complex conjugation."*

A mother is both real and imaginary.

I think I must understand simple math in order to understand the mother: how one multiplies and becomes two. How biological and psychological necessity keeps the mother and child attached as one, in their two bodies. How this generates complexity and as the child grows, becomes autonomous, the mother is left as a single being, desiring that the child remain a part of her. She, who created it in the first place.

It's clear that *mother* exists as an origin. As a begetter of life where life could not otherwise be. She is the denominator, the figure that which represents the total population, the thing *underneath the line*, below the fraction that divides the number above it.

I now understand that I am not a number, but a fraction of a number: ⅛:

One child of the eight my mother birthed, because one or three or seven were not enough for her.

Such a fraction could devalue my place as one whole person in the world. A mother who loves you gives you the full value of wholeness. A mother who does not will fracture you until you are one thousandth of a thousand wandering, wondering selves.

What I want to know is, why does a conjugate exist? A website says it can help you rationalize the denominator. It says, *remember this little trick, it may help you solve an equation one day.*

But the equation of mother is one I still can't solve for.

Einstein wrote, "Pure mathematics is, in its way, the poetry of logical ideas."

It's no surprise that I turned my mother into an idea. Transference of an affective experience into a conceptual one helps the thinker distance themselves from the origin of pain that brought them to ruminate the subject in the first place.

> (I could say something about pain here,
> but pain is not logical the way a cloud is
> not logical the way a war is not logical
> the way a motherless child is not.)

Richard Courant, mathematician and author of the book *What is Mathematics* described mathematics as "an expression of the human mind which reflects the active will, the contemplative reason, and the desire to aesthetic perfection." Its basic elements are:

> *logic*   (my mother cannot love me)
> *intuition*   (I have a feeling my mother does not love me)
> *analysis*   (my mother does not love me because _____)
> *construction*   (my mother made and then unmade me)
> *generality*   (all mothers love their children)
> *and individuality*   (I, alone, am unloved by my mother)

Basic elements help us understand the reason a thing exists. Such as pain existing because the mind and body exist. Like mathematics existing because of numbers. The way I exist because of my mother.

When my husband was still my husband, he read this and asked, do you *like* math now? "No," I said, then "yes." I meant there was more sense to it but not any complete, adequate meaning. The real answer is, I still don't understand it, though likability and understandability aren't mutually exclusive. I know it is possible to love something you don't understand, such as the sea. Or the thing that has gone from you. Or watching it go.

Bertrand Russell wrote, "I like mathematics because it is not human and has nothing particular to do with this planet or with the whole accidental universe—because, like Spinoza's God, it won't love us in return."

Mathematics, like my mother, doesn't love me enough to explain itself fully, though, unlike my mother, it is explicit in its desirability for a logical answer as to Y, (as to why):

$$X + Y \text{ becomes } X - Y$$

(child + mother becomes child − mother)

It helps you rationalize the denominator. But it doesn't change anything.

HALATION

To look is a simple action. To see, more difficult.

I think this one summer as I stare at childhood photos. I keep them out of sight. In one I see brothers and sisters: arms around arms around arms. It is them and it is me. We are almost, all together, not separate. In the photograph, light forms us. I think the mother took this photo, placed us here, this particular way. I wish that we had the light of knowing but instead we have this light: halation, a fog spreading us into each other. All of us her wounds in a row. None of us know yet. And what I eventually learn, the rest of them never seem to have to. Sometimes a mother just will not love you.

*

Halation is a scattering of light. As in "light that is improper" or "light that has spread beyond its natural boundaries." In other words, an error of light.

Is a mother an error when she cannot love her child? A malfunction of instinct? If she is not hard-wired. If she cannot feel shame. If she does not feel at all or feels hardly. If she can banish you. If she cannot love you. If she cannot love.

Would I still call her *Mother*? *other*? *her*?

*

Halation concerns a phenomenon of the eyes which spontaneously creates the effect of a gradient. Artist Gabriel Mott explains it using the metaphor of a family. He says, "A color awakens among its family and becomes aware of its surroundings" and then "two parent colors spread into each other achieving a child color. The child color vibrates a little and suddenly they all know about each other and become luminous."

*

Light is a temporary fiction. Like a story. I try to expose it through a specific lens and all I get is blur. What do I want? Not merely to tell the truth. I want the truth believed, like a hyper-focused image: sharp boundaries, clean grain, concrete and abstract meaning attainable.

It occurs to me I am trying to shed light *on* light. Light *on* the mother.

How entirely imperceptible.

*

As I write, I read a book called *Happily.* In it, the author claims: "If you ask what's under the apple skin you're exposing exposed-ness." (Hejinian)

I want there to be an image for you to see.

Look:

Children like fuzzy bulbs on the top of light poles. Their bright face-rings attached to dark bodies.

Halation: to make of the thing a halo.   Anagram: *anti-halo.*

Look:

Language, too, can be an optical illusion.

*

I wrote a book called *The Opposite of Light,* knowing it was an equation I could not solve. The reader will decide, I told myself. But my husband woke me up one January morning, cold as stone, and told me knowing answers to the questions I make is my burden alone.

He was light, my husband. A temporary fiction. Whatever knowing occurred in our twelve years together was a knowing born out of distance. I chased; he ran. A miracle we were ever in the same room together. Wrote Jacques Roubaud, "Light has already, while you were giving it boundaries, while you legislated the impossible, turned the corner."

*

When we married at City Hall in San Francisco, the mother was not there. It was the end of November and brightness poured through the rotunda on all sides.

Roubaud: "Light leads the eye beyond the where."

I would have loved him beyond any distance, to any *where*, if only I could see the where.

*

I've felt closer to the dark all my life. But light itself is not strange to me. It is the most commonly used expressions of light that I find most foreign:

light dawned
light dawned (on one)
as light as
the light of day
(and most enthusiastically)
the light of light of light of my life

Wrote a philosopher, "Our exposures to different seas and suns have changed us." (Barthes)

Wrote a poet, "Each child still has one lantern inside lit. May the Mother not Blow her children out." (Brock-Broido)

DERIVATION

I assign myself to a mountain so that I can unassign my pain. It is the *Zugspitze* or *Wildspitze*, I don't remember which. I go to it in search of largeness, its dome-dressed equivocal top. Because of this, and because of the mountain's size, I become very minor.

[It is into the tattering of praxis, I go.]

To my astonishment, the pain does not change. The force of the thought of it batters me like a wind rose at the highest peak.

On the way up, a man tells me they used to hide bombs in the plateau and I don't know if I should believe him. He carries a small knife by the blade, lets the handle glisten in the sun.

It is late spring, but the mountain still has snow. A heavy white, like when your eyes are closed.

[To escape the grammatical present, I must keep going back.]

I think, explosives explode. Then they are exploded, and thus, undangerous. Does the same go for language? I drag my boots through the *Schnee*, marking lines in every direction I go.

Aristotle wrote, "Objects which in themselves we view with pain, we delight to contemplate when reproduced with minute fidelity." I am trying to explode language. One would think this reverses its lashing, but the more time moves forward, the tighter pain screws into me.

[A mountain does nothing. Undoes nothing.]

"Mental steadfastedness," the man says, "is what it takes to survive." He's talking about extreme cold then an avalanche. "Jump up slope, beyond the fracture line. Move quickly to either side."

If I could move beyond the fracture I would. But all origin is bluish. We meander toward it like pilgrims to inevitable light. The man is not a guide, but a tourist like me. I walk away from him, head across the glacier toward the *Windloch*.

As I go, I pass a small stone chapel and sign:

Lass deine Fußspuren im ewigen Eis liegen. (Leave Your Footprints in Eternal Ice)

*

Back at the hotel, I want to believe something Aristotelian about myself if only to deduce that pain has an illustrative formula. Something like the syllogism: "All golden mountains are mountains, all golden mountains are golden, therefore some mountains are golden," which, according to research, suggests the existence of at least one golden mountain.

I write the following down in a notebook:

"If all pain is useful, and a shovel is a useful tool for digging, then all pain is a useful tool for digging."

[Aristotle: the irrational sometimes does not violate reason.]

I rarely remember the beginnings of anything, particularly of pain. It always appears in *media res*, when I am walking through a door, or swimming the sidestroke, or belly to belly with an old lover in a new town (the same reddening though, same turning sky). That I went to the mountain to leave something behind, that I don't remember which mountain, or how memory stings your legs the faster you walk backwards. It is quite probable that I am a poor harbinger with no sense of time; a witness to a thinking that exists spatially, not in sequence. I never know where I am in the pain, how much longer I have to go.

It is intractable whether I am on or off a mountain. One second the sunlight has me and then it does not. I am something other than what I am. What I am is something other.

[Post hoc ergo propter hoc]

57

We are heterological and I imagine we are riding backwards, all of us, the ones linked, causally, to my pain. We slope down to the base of it, back to the beginning. We crash at it or lash at it, depending on how impact is perceived.

I'm not historical, but I believe what Aristotle wrote: "to learn gives the liveliest pleasure." What have I learned?

Mountains last. Trees last. Bones last. Mothers and lovers do not.

[The present still lacerates me.]

Spring makes me dewy and I dislike its bulbs. Too much newness. All of this reminds me of that April day when I asked my husband (his one foot out the door):

Can you please freeze my sadness like a Russian winter bell so that it only rings in the past?

MULTIPLICATION

I learned the figure in school. The chemistry teacher used examples of soda cans, jolly ranchers, paper airplanes. How many mol of bicycles would it take to circle the earth? How many to reach from New York to the moon? Mol, a unit of measure equaling $6.02214065 \times 10^{23}$. Also called Avogadro's number, it's used to measure large quantities of very small entities, like atoms or molecules.

The figure, to me, is abstract. Large enough that my mind cannot comprehend its limits. I know it exists as a kind of translation; a way to move from the microscopic to the macroscopic. Something more tangible for the mind to grasp.

When I first met my husband, we fell in love immediately. It was fervent and startling. All I remember of those early days was our play of proximity: his body near to mine but always inches away, arching. The tousled bed covers. Smell of sweat. My neck spun with hair. Simulacrum of lovers. He was careful never to give me exactly what I wanted.

Upon waking, each morning, I'd ask him, "Do you love me?"

"*Yes*," he'd say.

"How much?" I'd respond.

"*Mol.*"

He loved me a large amount. That I knew. One mol of doughnuts would cover the entire earth in a doughnut layer five miles deep. My young self thought it was enough.

Towards the end of our marriage, he took me to the edge of a seaside cliff and told me to look at the endless, forever water. I think he meant it as a metaphor. I looked and stayed silent, didn't say to him what I was thinking. That somewhere on the other side of the ocean was a piece of land, surely ending it.

When I am alone, the infinitive strikes me senseless and it says go, go, as if action can berate you into an action. It is action that says to you—you cannot make this a memory, you cannot. This can only be a present action and you must wear it and never take it off.

[To sit in a room which is dark.]

To imagine light as a force-field.

To behave like the dark and travel in every direction.

To crack your knuckles while in a deep sleep.

To remember that bones will be all the earth keeps.

To consider the temporality of an apple.

To feel hungry all through the night.

To think a lover exists for the sound of their breathing.

To not think about the possibility of his leaving.

DECONSTRUCTION

I thought I could stop time by taking it apart. Something Derridean. Time reconstructed as a story. Beginning, middle, and end. An end to the pain. I wanted to find it.

When summer begins one June, I drive the New York thruway upstate to a large lake surrounded by trees. The water glows from the sun's rays and when I dive beneath the surface, I enter a different world. I cannot stay below, I know, but while underneath, I feel an odd keeping. Does the water want me or do I want it, I think to myself. I circle my arms to try and grasp it. An impossibility. But in this moment, I think if I never come up, the pain cannot have me. That I would be able to eschew it, remain in perpetual baptism.

Eventually, I give in to breath.

In her book *The Body in Pain*, Elaine Scarry writes that pain is the absolute definer of reality, and that its experience is purely singular. "Whatever pain achieves," she claims, "it achieves in part through its unsharability."

She's referring to physical as well as emotional pain. Trauma ravages the body. The spine becomes a stake in you. It holds you up, yes, but the nerves dotted up and down it burn like thousands of little fires. Your chest carries on it the heavy material of the past. Once, a few years back I went to the doctor, sure I had a tumor where my jaw meets my ear. The pain was unbearable, and I was having trouble hearing. "It's not your ear, it's the top of your jaw," she said with sternness in her eyes, "you must stop clenching your teeth when you sleep. The jaw is the most important hinge in the body, one you want to keep."

In water, you can be all mind. The body can disappear in its weightlessness, and with it, the pain.

When I tell a friend going through a trauma that she should start swimming, she asks if the muddled underwater world only exacerbates the brain's thinking. "Without sound, doesn't your mind become louder?" she asked.

No, I explained. The world becomes a mere echo and is so distant, it is like Derrida's *trace*, a track or path toward or away from. An absent presence. In it, your body becomes so body-less, so estranged from its own knowability, that you can imagine the pain leaking out of you, washed of you, going.

"But that is just your imagination," she said.

Pain is never imaginary. But it is not (as Scarry also claims) an object. You cannot throw it like a stone toward the sun, smash it in your hands, or leave it on a highway road.

She uses variables to outline this logic:

> " . . . desire is desire of x, fear is fear of y, hunger is hunger for z; but pain is not 'of' or 'for' anything—it is itself alone."

Maybe I've made a mistake. Maybe I'm trying to unmake a thing you simply can't unmake.

Pain equals pain, I thought, when I finally lifted my body from that lake.

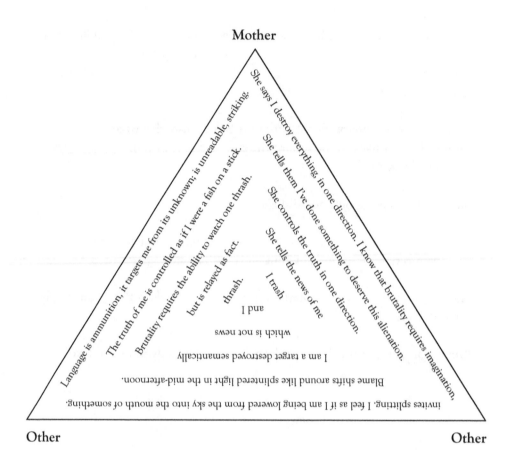

Mother

Other

Other

The triangle contains, reading around its edges:

She says I destroy everything, in one direction. I know that brutality requires imagination,

She tells them I've done something to deserve this alienation.

She controls the truth in one direction.

She tells the news of me

I trash

and I

thrash.

I pue

which is not news

I am a target destroyed semantically

Blame shifts around like splintered light in the mid-afternoon.

invites splitting, I feel as if I am being lowered from the sky into the mouth of something.

but is relayed as fact.

Brutality requires the ability to watch one thrash.

The truth of me is controlled as if I were a fish on a stick.

Language is ammunition, it targets me from its unknown; is unreadable, striking.

ACTION

I am asked by my editor to write a poem for a new anthology involving experimental forms. He calls it a mirror poem. "There must be an echo," he says. I sit in a chair for hours, measuring reflected words and sounds: *other, stuttered, known, blown, a, est, away.* Words circle as starlings, like a murmuration in which intricate patterns function as a potential threat to a threat. It shows that cohesion can be obtained in uncertain environments.

Mother is one. And I have, on occasion, been   *When*
painting, all year long, watercolor bruises. My   *I*
god, I couldn't write, so I thought it was civilized to sink   *think*
them into paper: an accomplishment, thereof,   *of*
translating pain into color. I would have preferred   *her*
a brush, not *a thing done*: mother who left me needing   *reading*
the internet for tips on how to live motherless.   *This*
disobedience was civilized. I let the water ride,   *I*
let the blue run, a behavior of illustration linked   *think*
back to the Renaissance, a history of motherlove: *of*
art depicting the sublime: the act of choosing (not)   *bruising*
your child. Though I was never hit, I am quite sure   *her*
acts of not-loving made of me an uncivilized design   *mind.*

DISINTEGRATION

Every September it feels the same. Shocks of memory render me back to that day: planes flying, buildings on fire, people jumping, the ghostly and the dead. All of us looped together in the horror.

"We changed in composition," a newscaster once said.

Composer John Cage wrote, "Form will be our only constant connection with the past." I improvise this memory, reform an imagined past:

> It is me that is there, halfway up one of these towers. The mother waits and waits for me, sits lowly on a couch twenty miles away. When I finally call to say I'm okay, that I've made it out, her body shivers with pronounceable joy. From then on, she loves me always.

This fictive memory is so appropriative that it must appear as delusion. I think I am one of those people who imagines a death I don't want, for a love I can't have. A desperate exchange.

*

The mother would not allow sound, so I watched replay after replay on silent; the TV box almost shook as the buildings soundlessly collapsed. I imagined the sound of screaming, the sound that dying makes. To this day, if I listen carefully, I can still hear everything disintegrate:

bodies, childhoods, marriages, families

It changed our composition.

Cage: "If there were a part of life dark enough to keep out of it a light from art, I would want to be in that darkness, fumbling around, if necessary, but alive."

To make art from pain is not original, but it is important. It's why we spend our lives with language, hoping one day, it renders us back. We call it *form* or *composition*: a layered and intentional trying. We put our names on it, send it into the world, hope someone can hear us.

*

I believe in silence because when I was a child no one heard me. Silence a childhood makes. Silence is what the mother gave me.

Cage did not believe in silence. He wrote, "There is no such thing as silence, get thee to an anechoic chamber and hear there thy nervous system in operation and hear there thy blood in circulation."

Every time I imagine myself dead, sound is the first thing to tell me I'm alive again.

*

Every fall, it's the same. I listen, on repeat, to William Basinski's *Disintegration Loops*, listen as the music fades into the darkening sky.

Cage: "Is the word, 'music' music?/ Does it communicate anything?/ Must it?/ If it's high, does it?/ If it's low, does it?/ If it's in the middle, does it?/ If it's soft does it?/ If it's loud does it?/ If it's an interval does it?/ What is an interval?/ Is an interval a chord?/ Is a chord an aggregate?/ Is an aggregate a constellation?/ What's a constellation?/ How many sounds together?/ One million?/ Ten thousand?/ Eighty-eight?"

Basinski, an avant-garde composer, is an artistic descendant of Cage. In the 1980's he made tapes of found sounds: "the clicking electric buses, grasshopper legs, trolleys creaking, the sound of coins dropping, the flutter of an oscillating fan." He called it "a sleepwalking mesh of horns and strings," and described it as, "just coming from the sky." He strung the sounds together on old magnetic tapes: constellated noise that sings its improvisation.

Cage: "The sound of a truck at fifty miles per hour. Static between the stations. Rain."

Twenty years later, Basinski took these old tapes and tried to convert them to digital: a modern transaction. But as the tape passed through the tape head, the backing detached and the film began to crumble, silvering off as it was fed. He let the tape loop through anyway, recording the sound of the music as it died. He finished the final transfer on September 11th, sat on his roof deck and filmed the smoke as it erased itself from the sky.

A change in composition.

*

Disintegration of the body is a body. Of childhood, it is a childhood. Of marriage, it is a marriage.

The thing itself becoming itself. As it dies, it is created.

But the disintegration of language is not a language. It is an erasure. If you are lucky, before it's gone, it becomes an elegy to everything that's been lost.

There is no alternative to the infinitive, even when it fails. One can say that it's time's main initiative to fly, but no one has ever said it has flown. The present can dislodge you from any future.

[To discover that the infinitive is a delusion.]

To invent a new conclusion.

To recognize no difference between *mother* and *other.*

To question what we take from another.

To be fascinated by sound.

To think shadows are overrated at noon.

To endure absence.

To erase any trace of a face.

To wonder how each action defines you.

ELIMINATION

I research poets who killed themselves. It is my second winter in the Midwest, and the long coldness has settled into my every living bone. I want to understand the option of death, not to be closer to it, but to remove the thought of it from my head completely. Its infinite straggling. I think death would be a chosen banishment, not imposed by the mother, but orchestrated by her: our collaboration of elimination.

It is thought, unverifiably, that she died in a leap off the white rock of Leukas (for love): "I simply want to be dead. Weeping she left me/ with many tears and said this: Oh how badly things have turned out for us."

Sappho

Described her despair as "an owl's talons clenching my heart" found dead with her head in the oven, the room sealed off: "The woman is perfected./ Her dead/ body wears the smile of accomplishment."

Sylvia Plath

Hanged herself in Yelabuga, 1941: "и под землею скоро уснем мы все,/ кто на земле не давали уснуть друг другу": "And soon all of us will sleep under the earth, we / who never let each other sleep above it."

Marina Tsvetaeva

1929. Paris, France. He used a ruler to be sure the bullet would pass right through his heart. Book titles include: *Et puis Merde!* and *Agence Générale du Suicide.*

Jacques Rigaut

Aboard the steamship *Orizba*, he was beaten for making sexual advances toward a man and threw himself overboard into the Gulf of Mexico: "The bells, I say, the bells break down their tower;/ And swing I know not where."

Hart Crane

He shot himself in the head in New York City, 2007: "At 13/ I find out Mom had been doing years/ In a federal prison all that time,/ For stealing, so no mental hospital for/ Mommy. Breakdown ours alone./ I was on my own."

Liam Rector

She was (in her words) "drawn to the suffering of Baudelaire, the suicide of Nerval, the premature silence of Rimbaud" and overdosed on secobarbital sodium after a short, difficult life: "Coger y morir no tienen adjectivos.": "To fuck and to die have no adjectives."

Alejandra Pizarnik

Drowned himself in the Seine. Parents died in Nazi death camps while he was imprisoned into forced labor, clearing the debris of a post office and burning Russian books: "Die Nachzustotternde Welt": "World to be stuttered by heart/ in which/ I shall have been a guest, a name/ sweated down from the wall/ a wound licks up."

Paul Celan

It was reported, on returning home one evening, "she put on her mother's fur coat, removed all her rings, poured herself a glass of vodka, locked herself in the garage, and started the engine of her car": "I'm tired of faces that I don't know/ and now I think that death is starting./ Death starts like a dream,/ full of objects and my sister's laughter."

Anne Sexton

Shot himself in the chest, left a partially finished poem behind: "And so they say—'the incident dissolved'/ the love boat smashed up/ on the dreary routine./ I'm through with life/ and [we] should absolve from mutual hearts, afflictions and spleen."

Vladimir Mayakovsky

His rumored last words were "Messy, aint it?" though this is unconfirmed. Shot himself with a .44 magnum, body not found for a month. Said, "All of us have a place in history. Mine is clouds."

Richard Brautigan

She overdosed on sleeping pills in 1933: Did not leave
this poem as a suicide note, as believed, but published
it 18 years prior: "When I am dead and over me bright
April/ Shakes out her rain-drenched hair,/ Tho' you
should lean above me broken-hearted,/ I shall not
care./ I shall have peace, as leafy trees are peaceful/
When rain bends down the bough,/ And I shall be
more silent and cold-hearted/ Than you are now."

Sara
Teasdale

REACTION

When I think of her reading this, I think of bruising her mind.

CALCULATION

You walk, every day, along shaded sidewalks, counting *one two, one two*. And you know it's true, the mother cannot calculate you.

But you can calculate her.

She is one: One planet. One massive sphere. A center. A home.
                                          A governing body.

It's what she always wanted: to be the one:

     one gravitational center that pulls and is pulled
     and connects all that surrounds her:

     one mother planet to her moons: one thing on its sky-throne
     with the many bowing things before it.

My mother is a planet with too many moons.

The brother and sister moons all reflected light back to her and so she became addicted to the light. The moons saw this and knew they must keep making it if they were to be loved and held and kept. They war with each other, up into adulthood, to give the mother what she expects. Imagine: eight moons revolving and resolving to be the one main moon to the mother planet. To be the one, when one-ness isn't attainable. To war with the other moons. The mother wants this war, it keeps her living.

one

two

three

four

war war war

five

six

seven

eight

take take take

A mother can teach you to count, to calculate her.

Research shows the earth's moon formed when a large collision tore a chunk of Earth away.

The outermost crust is broken and jumbled due to all the large impacts it has received. Known, in other words, as *a shattered zone*.

Research shows the moon's gravitational pull may have been key to making Earth a livable planet by moderating the degree of wobble in the planet's axial tilt.

"The moon doesn't escape from this action unscathed," it says, "the Earth's gravity stretches the moon into its odd shape."

Though you are a moon, in all your moon-ness, you are not a moon she wants. Though she raised you as she raised the other moons. You are round and arced just like the others. You run your hand along your brutal moon-shape and think the roundness might mean something.

It does not.

"Nothing is so sure as the sun," a stranger once told me, referencing my sunburnt skin, hot pink and warm. He reached out his fingers to touch me. You must be brave now, I think. Brave as that stranger touching surety, he thinks.

[Not to underestimate mathematical functions.
To expect them to reestablish some direction
for thinking, for exploding dormant certitudes.]

To never arrive at a theory.

To try and try again.

To swim against the current in La Jolla
as the rain hits your back.

To think a back is a fragile thing.

To be endlessly surprised by cruelty.

To compress your needs into a small ball.

To, like Sisyphus, learn resistance.

INTERROGATION

Was I waiting for . . .

Did I expect her to . . .

Had I assumed that she . . .

Why wasn't there . . .

Why isn't there a . . .

Had somewhere I . . .

Did the result mean . . .

Where was my . . .

Is there a . . .

When did she . . .

Why did she . . .

Why can't there be . . .

How is that . . .

How come she could . . .

What can I . . .

Why didn't she . . .

Why did she . . .

How could I . . .

How could I not . . .

ERADICATION

/ɪˌradɪˈkeɪʃ(ə)n. English, 16th century, comes from *eradictus*, the past participle of the Latin "radix" meaning root:

"to pull up by the roots"
"to pull up by her roots"
"to pull up by my roots"

Synonyms: abolish, annihilate, black out, blot out, cancel, efface, erase, expunge, obliterate, root (out), snuff (out), stamp (out), sweep (away). See also: extirpation, disambiguation.

*

A therapist asks me what I might have gained from all of this? I don't know how to answer the question. "Everything is lost," I say. "Well, then what have you lost?" I don't know how to answer the question. "Make a list," he says, "Draw a box on a piece of paper and put everything you've lost inside it."

> She took with her a home, the concept of home, a dog, child-
> hood windows, old March snow. A history and stories,
> a clock turning forward and forward, melon in the morning.
> Brothers and sisters, a beach, a way to reach them, a way
> to be conditional: if, all my ifs, the way hope can live inside
> letters, she took, the first flicker of a new life, a daughter
> I'm afraid I'll never want. The knock knock knock
> (are you there?) of my head against that loss. How I sound
> with grief. She took relief and learning and left me
> constantly turning toward a massive, lashing rain. Gave me
> pain and pain and pain and pain. A whole line of repetition
> which sprang me mathematically into action. She gave me
> one final subtraction: a sad knowledge that I know is true:
> the same world that mothers you, unmothers you too.

*

The sonnet is a fascist form, or so it is rumored that a poet had said so.

Rita Dove describes the sonnet as a *heile Welt* or "intact world" in the preface to her book *Mother Love*. She writes, "Everything is in sync, from the stars down to the tiniest mite on a blade of grass. And if the true sonnet reflects the music of spheres, it then follows that any variation represents a world gone awry."

"Can't form be a talisman against disintegration?" she asks.

*

It is thought a poet invented fascism, an aesthetic ideology to counter the ennui of Italian democratic structure circa 1900, one that pushed a romanticized vision of order and war.

This poet, Gabriele D'Annunzio wrote sensually and beautifully of Abruzzo (where he was born) and of his lover (known by the pseudonym Ermione):

E immerse
noi siam nello spirto silvestre,
d'arborea vita viventi;
e il tuo vólto ebro
è molle di pioggia come una foglia

And we are
Immersed in the spirit
Of the woodland,
Alive with arboreal life;
And your ecstatic face
Is soft with rain
As a leaf

Also a soldier and political figure, D'Annunzio became a member of the Arditi during the first world war, gave stylized, inflammatory speeches from balconies, and popularized the Roman salute (which was then adopted by the Nazis). He was known to pour castor oil down his adversaries' throats, a precursor to the future torture practices of Mussolini. D'Annunzio believed in "superior" humans, (including poets, prophets, and heroes), and famously said, "The rule for an intellectual is this: own, don't be owned."

Once, when I compared my family to a fascist regime, the therapist gave me a wide-eye and changed the subject. I don't think it's that he did not believe me, but that the overly sensationalized metaphor then sensationalized me. I became an exaggeration to him, a *dame floraison* who thinks, mostly, in metaphor. But it's true, no matter the problems of verisimilitude, no matter fixed societal archetypes, no matter the appearance of the mind's florid blooming: in this family I had no rights.

*

"No one can tell a mother how to act: / there are no laws when laws are broken, no names / to call upon. Some say there's nourishment for pain, and call it philosophy." (Dove)

*

The following week the therapist takes the paper back, says he likes my list and thinks it's quite musical. He doesn't recognize it as a sonnet. "It fits nicely in the box," he says, "you can leave it all in there, see, inside the closed walls of the square." He counts the things I've lost and asks me again, "now what have you gained?"

*

"This alone is what I wish for you: knowledge / to understand each desire has an edge, / to know we are responsible for the lives / we change." (Dove)

When I'm in a state of wonder, the infinitive *to wonder* extends the state across all place and time. I am not lost, but hiding within it and it should be strange, shouldn't it? It should. How strange.

[To gaze in wonder at cruelty.]

To trace pain back to the beginning of time.

To find yourself inarticulate.

To loot someone else's sentences.

To escape movement in sleep.

To wake and paint another bruise.

To wish for his hips five hours per night.

To try not to read the news.

EDUCATION

Que sais-je?

Some days, just this story:

In Rong-cheng, China, at the Shendiaoshan wildlife reserve, a baby elephant was born and shortly after nearly stomped to death by his mother.

Eventually, the zookeepers removed the baby from the enclosure in order to save his life.

Faced not just with the rejection of his mother, but the physical separation from her, the little elephant wept uncontrollably for hours, tears streaming down his swollen baby face.

You can see, on various websites, a photo of him lying under a gray blanket, exhausted, mouth agape. He is devastated, inconsolable.

During my research, I come across surveillance footage of the mother lifting her large hooves to him. Fast-forward a bit, it says, and you can hear him, now alone, weep for her.

I have learned enough not to watch it.

DEFORMATION

What feels unfathomable floats down me slowly like a silver leaf to the bottom of my mind. Loss is a curious system. It allows for burnishing.

I thought, in writing this, I'd be erasing loss, but realize now I'm trying to harden the softest parts of it. Smooth it. Gleam it. The force of this process elasticizes all I thought was firmly true.

I assemble language to disassemble meaning—or I disassemble language in order to reassemble meaning—this is all an effort to estrange the ordinary: a pair of socks, the name of that place, subway car, chair or shadow, the front of a sparrow, something afloat like, a naked rock.

The result is something new.

For two years, I've watched a construction crew slowly deconstruct a house. Plank by plank, they removed its center, its sides, leaving only the front-flat structure like a headless face. Through its windows, all you can see is blue sky. Every day that I walk by it, I glare at its deformed state, look into it as if into a mirror. Sometimes I cry.

It's true that I'm afraid of formlessness. That the world, for me, is contingent on shape. It's why I love language. Like loss, it allows for burnishing.

There are three kinds of deformation:

1. *Elastic*—wherein the strain is reversible

2. *Ductile*—wherein the strain is irreversible

3. *Fracture*—wherein the material breaks

A year after the mother had exiled me, I held, in Italy, a freshly grown pomegranate in my hand, its spherical shape round like a little world. Though not a world I needed. I was like Persephone tying myself to the underworld. Except there was no Demeter to stop the fruits of the earth from growing. Everything in the world remained bountiful, it seemed, except for me.

It was in this moment I made a promise to myself. If I wanted to die, I had to wait until age forty. After that, I'd no longer owe the world my living.

This was my point of fracture.

While trying to forget the shape of this moment, the pomegranate like a world in my hands, I repeat the word *sphere* over and over until it becomes estranged from itself:

> *sphere*
> *sphere*
> *sphere*
> *sphere*
> *sphere*
> *sphere*
> *spheres*
> *spheres*
> *spheres*
> *spheres*
> *spheres*
> *spheres*
> *fears*
> *fears*
> *fears*
> *fears*
> *fears*
> *fears*
> *fears*
> *fears*
> *fears*
> *fear is*
> *fear is*
> *fear is*
> *fear is*

"People's mouths are brutal portable things," writes Lisa Robertson. Mine is no exception. While doing this exercise, I wonder if I am deforming language because of power, simply because I can. Because language is here, and I have control of it; its meanings and sounds malleable like the soft top of a baby's skull.

I have a reoccurring dream that I am stuck inside an elevator where an explosive device has been planted. The elevator is not stationary but moving up and up at a rate so slow, the ticking surpasses its movement. Going up takes 1,000 ticks and there is no way to know when the direction will shift. No numbers to count. No floors. Just an endless moving up inside four walls. A forever ticking and my life measured by the slow and quickness of it all.

The mother has been like this: a bomb in my life, though, unexploded and ticking my life away. A poor metaphor. Even unethical. But when I repeat the word "bomb" over and over to dull its power, all I end up with is her:

bomb

bomb

bomb

bomb

bomb

bomb

bomb

bomb

bomb

bomb

bomb

bomb

bomb

bomb

bomb

bomb

bomb

bomb

bomb

bomb

bomb

bomb

bomb

mom

mom

mom

mom

mom

mom

mom

mom

mom

mom

mom

mom

mom

I want to say goodbye to the mother at this point. But I know that is not possible. So I try to conjure up a different image:

violets

violets

violets

violets

violets

violets

violets

violets

violets

violets

violets

violets

violets

violets

violets
violets
violets
violence
violence
violence
violence
violence
violence
violence
violence
violence
violence
violence
violence
violence
violence
violence
violins
violins
violins
violins

CONCATENATION

A series of interconnected things, events, joining character strings end to end like a plaything.

*

When something is an origin, one attaches the word *mother* to it:

motherboard,   *mothership,*   *motherland.*

When a rule is absolute, one calls it a *mother-rule*, the *mother of all rules.*

*

In the Nangarhar province of Afghanistan, mothers walk in conflict, nine streams balance against a brutal, lowing sun. Time splits each instance and somewhere in the distance, the sound of a dayereh.

Then my motherland drops a bomb from overhead—the largest non-nuclear bomb ever dropped by the U.S.: called MOAB: *Mother Of All Bombs*

We are, all of us, undetachable from the violence of our mother.

*

meanwhile footprints allover
meanwhile caretaker lifelike
throwaway scapegoat overboard
background backlash everywhere
everything without footnotes
foreclosed brainwashed tenfold
fishbowl something blacklist forever
thereafter handmade lifeboat
somehow goodnight somehow
newfound afterimage

Infinite straggling is how to describe a day that will not come, and it is silly to think that it is coming. The infinitive tells us that nothing is coming; it is what's being done today. It is how the present remains an action, and us within it.

[To remain in doubt.]

To come together and apart.

To know sequence is about history.

To drive across the country.

To find Nebraska unbearable.

To trace the skimming yellow of cornfields against the sky.

To know a line can't mourn you.

To think road trips are a marital experiment.

To wake in Nevada to truck horns and a dust storm.

INTERPELLATION

Everywhere I've been my entire life, the same idea has been presented to me like some undeniable, steadfast fact: all mothers love their children. Without reserve or complication. Love that is unconditional, instinctual, pure, unwavering. Walk into any store around Mother's Day, the greeting card selection will tell you so.

This is the myth of the mother. The relationship is, always, one of hierarchy. The mother, for many years, maintains all power over the child, can choose what that power means; exert it with love and care or disregard and pain.

This is what I know is true: when power systems recognize an I—an I itself is recognized. This is how we become a subject. The conscious mind subjugates.

The unconscious mind learns that ideas moderate us. Then learns, in defense, how to moderate ideas.

*

"**Mother** is the name for **God** in the lips and hearts of little children." (William Makepeace Thackeray)

    Mother-God.

"The heart of a **mother** is a deep **abyss** at the bottom of which you will always find forgiveness." (Honoré de Balzac)

    Mother-abyss

"A **mother's** arms are made of **tender**ness and children sleep soundly in them." (Victor Hugo)

    Mother's end

"**Mother**hood: All love **beg**ins and ends there." (Robert Browning)

    Mother, beg

"We are born **out of love**: Love is our mother." (Rumi)

Out of love

"The love of a **mother** is the **veil** of a softer light between the heart and the heavenly Father." (Samuel Taylor Coleridge)

Mother-veil

"I miss thee, my **Mother**! Thy **image** is still/ The deepest /impressed on my heart." (Eliza Cook)

Mother-image

"Whatever else is unsure in this **stinking** dunghill of a world a **mother**'s love is not." (James Joyce)

Stinking mother

"The **mother**'s **heart** is the child's schoolroom." (Henry Ward Beecher)

Mother-art

"God could not be **everywhere**, therefore he made **mothers**." (Rudyard Kipling)

Everywhere, mothers

*

I am inadjectival. The pain cannot be explained.

To do is done, to fuck is fucked, to know is known, to think is thought, to configure is a figure, to find is found. I think to cry is to howl, I think, as I say to myself: *have the verbs that have you back.* Have them. We use the verb *to have* to indicate a marriage of sorts.

[To do as if things mattered.]

To fuck the one you love in New York,
California, Mexico, and Rome
while feverish and hungry and barely awake.

To know the brushstrokes a body makes.

To think they are permanent.

To configure an algorithm for thinking.

To find a new city more habitable than home.

To think of the mother's speech.

To cry every single night of the week.

TENDERIZATION

When Tom Petty comes on the radio, it has just snowed a foot and I can no longer remember the subtlety of California winters. I drive so slowly that ice formations shaped like little stars begin to form on the windshield, obstructing my view. I miss palm trees, their layered exuberance flayed, all winter, toward the sun. I miss the west coast's late February and the warm noon that carries itself into the early dark of March. Inklings of spring. I am on my way home from the supermarket to cook a meal after many months of depression, frozen pizza, no eating at all.

Tom sings the following sentence just as I pull into the driveway: "She's a good girl, loves her mama."

I shut the car off, breathe loudly. Does this mean if I no longer love my mother, that I am not good? Not a good girl? Never a good girl again? The questions sting at me as I carry the bags from the car into the kitchen.

Since when was goodness measured by our affection for our mothers? I wonder out loud to the empty room. Since when was goodness measured at all?

The recipe calls for three chicken breasts, pounded down to similar sizes. This is so they cook evenly. I don't have a meat mallet, so I use the backside of a frying pan. Pound to the rhythm of *good good good*. What I am not.

Would a good daughter write all of this or keep it to herself, like some martyr responsible for upholding the myth of mothers: that they all love without reservation, without condition, with a goodness bestowed to them as living-earth-angels, incapable of harm or any form of badness?

"Think tenderize. Not pulverize," the recipe says. But I do not think, at this moment, I am capable of tenderness.

Break it down. Make it softer—good good good.

I cannot do the work of the martyr, no matter how much I wish I could. The story must be told, not for harm, but for my own goodness, in my own eyes. The trauma story recognized, then reconstructed in order to survive.

I put the beaten chicken in a pan, cover it with the spices the recipe calls for, and close the oven door behind it. I've cleaved it so thin, it looks like the sad skin of a rabbit and likely won't taste any good. Still, in this moment, I'm thankful to the chicken for allowing me to pound it. For giving me a moment of violence. That I could hold it up and examine the result of my action: a mirror to my *ungoodness*.

Simone Weil wrote, "The great sorrow of human life is knowing that to look and to eat are two different operations." And that "children already experience this sorrow when they look at a cake for a long time and nearly regret eating it, but are powerless to help themselves."

This is a metaphor for the difficulty of telling. To hold the story or to release it. To consume it yourself or let it be consumed. To save yourself or your mother's own image. How each action transforms the story, who the story belongs to, how the story continues to exist as necessity or pleasure or pain. How you desire it, even require it—hungry for truth.

Weil: "Maybe the vices, depravities and crimes are nearly always or even always in their essence attempts to eat beauty, to eat what one can only look at. Eve initiated this. If she lost our humanity by eating a fruit, the reverse attitude—looking at a fruit without eating it—must be what saves."

I remove the chicken from the oven, burn my hand badly on the rack, and curse myself loud enough for the neighbors to hear: *You are such a fucking motherfucking cruel and stupid brute.*

It is not until much later that I wonder: is writing the truth or *not* writing it, akin to eating the fruit?

REPETITION

Twice I am located near death and the mother does not call. I think, do I exist?

> [Gertrude Stein: but the strange thing about the realization of
> existence is that like a train moving there is no realization of
> its moving if it does not move against something]

Twice I am located near death and twice the mother does not call. Sirens loom perpetual.

> [Gertrude Stein: is there repetition or is there insistence]

Twice I am located near death. I think, I do exist. That all thinking is an entrance. The mother does not call.

> [Gertrude Stein: I'm inclined to believe there is no such thing
> as repetition]

In one instance, the sirens loom perpetual, in their sonorous American way. In another, the violent ground shakes: *terremotto! terremotto!* A chorus of voices: *tenere tenere tenere le pareti!*

> [Gertrude Stein: expressing any thing there can be no repetition
> because the essence of that expression is insistence]

In an American way, a gunman enters a bank one mile from my home. One instance. Sirens loom perpetual. The shooter kills three. Many call to check on me but the mother does not.

> [Gertrude Stein: if you insist you must each time use emphasis]

Do I exist? Twice I am located near death and think I must have become a myth. The mother does not call. The earth shifts a bit on its axis, plates fall. The Umbrian ground undulates in its sonorous way.

> [Gertrude Stein: if you use emphasis is it not possible while
> anybody is alive that they should use exactly the same
> emphasis]

The mother does not call. In my head I invent her grin. The floor lamp shake-shifts, breaks the bulb of itself against the door. Am I the subject of myth?

> [Gertrude Stein: *That is what makes life that the insistence is different, no matter how often you tell the same story if there is anything alive in the telling the emphasis is different*]

Sirens loom perpetual. The news is wide for a day, then disappears in its American way. Workers mop up the blood at the entrance to the bank. The city slightly shifts, then resumes its undulating.

> [Gertrude Stein: *You listen as you know*]

The mother does not call. Has not called in years. You think you might exist but the sound of her voice is now the sound of myth.

> [Gertrude Stein: *Remembering is repetition anyone can know that*]

What is the threshold of remembering? Twice I was located near death. The mother did not call. Memory is the entrance of action. It looms perpetual. In my head, I invent her grin. The bulb of me breaks against the floor.

> [Gertrude Stein: *What one repeats is the scene in which one is acting, the days in which one is living, the coming and going which one is doing, anything one who is remembering is a repetition*]

So I let the power of her commence, there is no threshold for remembering. Actions loom perpetual. I think aesthetically: the Umbrian sky warp and weft with greenblues. Place is a thing of myth. So undulating. I shift.

> [Gertrude Stein: *The composition we live in changes but essentially what happens does not change*]

The self rotates on its axis, indeterminate. The sky, American in its own way, widens with news. In my head I invent a myth: I am dead and the mother shakes perpetually, like a violent quake. Her sonorous cries zig-zag from afar, then disappear.

[Gertrude Stein: We inside us do not change but our emphasis
and the moment in which we live changes]

Twice I am located near death and twice the mother does not call. All thinking is an entrance. The earth shifts a bit. I imagine her zig-zagging her arms from afar: power, commence.

[Gertrude Stein: There was the moving and the existence of
each moment as it was in me]

The mother does not call. Never calls. In my head, I invent her grin. There is no threshold for remembering. Her arms zig-zag from afar, conducting my pain: wave, wave.

ABSTRACTION

I came to the page for a defense against logic because logic let me down. It's not language I want. I want to be scrutable, like some barbarous flower shaped into a nerve ending.

If you look at me, you'll see the lines never oblige. You'll see an unrecognizable classification; a smudge of what once was *felt* life.

The truth is, pain designed me. It was an activity of consequence, orchestrated by abstraction. Hilma af Klint understood. For years she painted ideas, distanced them from objects: two swans twisted into a star, a planet called *Dove* (but no dove), and *Chaos:* half an ostrich against a dark-dark sky.

If only we could diagram marvelous insignificance:

—a circle in a circle in an eye in a pie—

Klint knew the world wasn't ready and so stored her work away for a future time.

I have this theory that every sentence weeps openly and once someone tries to understand it, the weeping stops.

Language switched on me bare-backed and I jumped. It wanted me more and fastly (to be as the Latin *abstrahere*) "drawn and pulled away":

a horse held and leading toward   the substituted shape of some *thing*.

DRAMATIZATION

Husband, do you remember?

In Florence, our sentences were short. We spoke in fractures. Were bewildered by daylight. Nightjars through the lunette. Spent mornings circling each other's navels, our fingers slow and distinctly bereft. This is when I knew love had left.

*

There comes a time when all thought must be unassailable.

> *I am the centre of*
> *A circle of pain*
> *Exceeding its boundaries in every direction.*
> (Mina Loy)

*

I found myself surreally living inside it, some sanctimonious star, let my points rip into him as though he'd absorb me. "I was built for pain," he told me in front of Botticelli's Venus (it did not astound), the corridors of The Uffizi led us around and around.

> *When pain surpassing itself becomes exotic.*
> (Mina Loy)

*

In the small dream, we lived automatic (not *"young lovers hermetically buttoned up in black"*) and fashioned a fictious whispering around art. The place is the witness to the witnessing. In the bathroom stall, our mouths fettered like gold, unchangeable. Automatically I said, "right here, it is you that I want."

> *Fleshes like weeds*
> *Sprout in the light.*
> (Mina Loy)

*

The large dream is a knot. In the piazza, there was a merging. We found, in the square, a corner, inside, a street, inside, a theater, inside, a film: watched a man scale the *Duomo*, motorcycle through Florence, end in Venice. When we walked from our seats and into the night, the octagonal dome shown above and ahead of us became our moon-in-real-life.

> I must traverse
> Traversing myself
> (Mina Loy)

*

When we tired of vaulted ceilings we retired with vaulted lungs; imagine sex or singing or holding your breath. He said, "Your skin is starry, sunless and spectral" and the lights the lights of that city largely wept.

I can't say it:

> We might have lived together
> In the lights of the Arno
> Or gone apple stealing under the sea
> Or played
> Hide and seek in love and cob-webs
> And a lullaby on a tin-pan.
> (Mina Loy)

*

Is this the traversing of pain? Morning found me faster than a dream. I went for a coffee by the Ponte Vecchio, hungry for croissants

> or breakfasting on rain.
> (Mina Loy)

*

It was darkly cold the day we left:

> I don't care
> Where the legs of the legs of the furniture are walking to

Or what is hidden in the shadows as they stride.
(Mina Loy)

It is his face I keep seeing, its blurring into, *focus focus*, our final Italian room. Love was the last wind the walls blew. And the sea, nowhere near us, shined out.

CONSOLATION

Mother me, mind

IMAGINATION

Can you imagine? I've used the phrase more times than are countable. I, in my desperation to have people understand, beg of them to use their faculties, not as a mechanism of empathy or transference, but a mechanism of knowing. I want them to know what it feels like. *Can you imagine?* I do not mean it rhetorically. I mean, if you are one who has been loved by your mother, can you imagine being jettisoned by her instead?

Or a husband you think will love you forever, who makes you tea, rubs your back, *can you imagine*, you wake up one day, he's gone, and it's the last? Some can, I'm sure. I cannot. I cannot imagine these things, these things that have happened. I cannot translate them into value or live anywhere that is not the mind.

When I was briefly outside of mine, it was late summer and in-between the afternoon heat and haze, a morning chill would rush through me and it was so startling, I thought I could see it. Actually see it. The cold settling itself into, off of, the morning clouds like soft hair strung from their bottoms.

The weather is not important, except that it is what I remember. How the chill felt on my arm-hairs. The sensorium in control. The rest lives inside images, lost and reproduced from somewhere else, outside of the intellect. A place I know but cannot distinguish as truth.

"Resistance," Wallace Stevens wrote, "is the opposite of escape."

In my imagination, fragments resist:

> Sunflowers by the house twice as tall as the trees.
> A wooden bench leading toward the sea.
> A mother folding laundry in the dim midnight light.
> She is larger than the sea.
> Her face is the middle of the sunflowers.
> She shakes in the breeze.
> The light leading toward the sea.
> A wooden mother folding down the middle.
> She is large and dim. Like a house.

Scale is the world as you remember it. "Reality is things as they are." But that only works in the present tense. Anything that has happened is remembered and memory is an activity of the imagined.

Barthes wrote a whole book based off a haunting photograph of his mother. "A ghost story," an article calls it. After losing her, he looked for her in old photographs, finding, repeatedly, that each image, no matter how similar, is lost of her person. But he describes one photo in-depth of his mother, age five, the only image he found of her true likeness. In a journal about this discovery he wrote the following words: "Je pleure."

"There are nightmares," he says in another book, "in which the Mother appears, her face hardened into a cold and severe expression. The fade-out of the loved object is the terrifying return of the Wicked mother, the inexplicable retreat of love, the well-known abandonment of which the Mystics complain: God exists, the Mother is present, but they no longer love. I am not destroyed, but dropped here, a reject."

If I've been trying to escape the mother, I've had it all wrong. She has escaped me. I am, in my mind, doing only what I can to resist her. The reality of her. Her goneness. It is like the iris in a reverie trembling in its awakeness, unable to actually see. Close-up on it and you'll notice, reflected in the pupil, a face.

Brutality requires imagination. I've seen it. The old life transfigured with the new. The family around the dinner table, a daughter missing. She is in a field far away behaving like the clouds. Appearing and disappearing. Her wedding ring is in the dirt and her body is sprawled out like a star.

Nobody ever really knows where you are.

Stevens wrote, "It is one of the peculiarities of the imagination that it is always at the end of an era. What happens is that it is always attaching itself to a new reality and adhering to it. It is not that there is a new imagination but that there is a new reality."

In this reality, I live eventually. As in, a life that doesn't work but maybe one day will. One, I imagine, where the mother no longer exists, or her image can be replaced with the likeness of someone other.

This reminds me of a film I can't remember the name of where the lover says to another, "Beautiful to leave you here" and then the screen fades to black. From nowhere, off screen, you hear a voice whispering, "and where precisely is that?"

FICTION

The first time I spent Christmas alone, I read Mary Shelley's *Frankenstein* on the beach in a Mexican port village. It rained for two days straight, and I lay in it while people shielded themselves under canopies. They watched me with curiosity. I transformed to them, became a little less human; woman who allows the rain to have her. (And look, she doesn't even flinch).

I was too mesmerized by the book to care. Shocked at how wrong I had it. I'd always thought Frankenstein *was* the monster, made with good intentions by a man who wished to animate a thing to life. But now I understand that Victor, the story's narrator, *is* Frankenstein. His monster, the character we have come to familiarize with his surname, is never referred to as anything but *creature* and its synonyms.

Victor Frankenstein's desire to explore the unknown mysteries of creation is preceded by three profound events: first, his father dismisses his interest in a book by German theologian Heinrich Cornelius Agrippa, one of the "lords" of Victor's imagination. Second, he witnesses a tree electrocuted by lightning ("It was not splintered by shock, but entirely reduced to thin ribbons of wood") during a terrible thunderstorm in Geneva. "I never beheld anything so utterly destroyed," he said.

Then his mother dies, ("My internal being was in a state of insurrection and turmoil: I felt that order would thence arise, but I had no power to produce it") and it's in the midst of this grief he begins his creation.

"Nothing is so painful to the human mind as a great and sudden change." Nothing so painful as loss. And how suddenly the mind desires order after it. A form for continuing.

It is these events that also facilitate his ruin. Victor is admonished at the "catastrophe" of his creation and runs from it, only to be faced with the greatest of ironies. The monster, who was not created "bad" but becomes bad because of his exclusion from the world, suffers, and so decides his creator will suffer too. Thus, a series of events unfold toward Victor Frankenstein's own psychological demise.

It is not lost on me, what I am doing. Putting this down into language. But I realize, now, that the mother's actions have not been all about power (as I thought they were). They are also about loneliness. Do not tell me becoming a mother is not about both. That a mother never thought, as Shelley wrote, "a new species would bless me as its creator and source; many happy and excellent natures would owe their being to me;" so that she would not have to feel, as the creature in the story felt: the indefatigable solitariness of humanhood.

I imagine this was my mother's thinking. She who dreamt of making life but didn't like what she made. I feel the harshest truth of this fact: I am her failed creation.

Of course, she would tell you a different story.

*

When there was a sudden brightness of the periphery, I lifted my head to see the horizon and thought the rain had stopped, but it had become just a mix of light and water. I was unsure what waiting for "good" weather meant and if it could ever be truly good. If the sun expanded itself into the sky and the rain disappeared, my skin would have burned itself into welts and I would have had no choice but to cover myself from its light.

"Destroy your own creature" is what I'm trying to do. An act of decreation. And I must get on with it. How else will I ever believe in human goodness?

Under the sky and split shadows of the palms, I cried hard because my marriage was over. Because I was losing sight of my mother. And time kept moving on.

The first time I saw her, I could not say. I was a tiny body pulled from an incision in hers. No intellect yet. No machine for memory. But the last time I saw her, I will not forget. She stood her body in the doorway of that house, a home as one had ever so been, and I knew, I knew I would never get back in.

Pain is an instrument of my life. Unlike Victor Frankenstein, I do not think my grief is an indulgence, though I indulge it. It is a necessity to me. Writing this is a duty I have to perform. What else would I do with my pain? Where to put it but set it down into language?

FRUSTRATION

I collect all my essay attempts together and call them my rectangles of failure.

Little graveyard of what I could not make.

*Redaction

1.   I think the mother thinks

[redacted]

3.   that I know I am

*Causation

cause   effects,   cause
effects

*Recollection

to remember

how language
escapes
time how
time escapes
language how
a mother
left
verbatim

*Intermodulation

Freud: "The voice of the intellect is a soft one,
but it does not rest until it has gained a hearing."

*Evocation

I imagine her telling
me *don't be
elliptical*—a word
        she   does   not
know

*Desperation

know, I'd give up all rhetoric for love

*Recognition

Freud: "from error to error
one discovers the truth."

*Alteration

an artist I know from Mexico
made drawings of memory-
-less leaves\ chaotic green—lines
squiggled everywhere—

they have forgotten what they are, she
said.

The etymological root of word *infinitive* means eternal, limitless. In case you were wondering if language ever closes anything.

[*To cross the threshold.}*

To understand permanence.

To carefully compose every hard sentence.

To know the absoluteness of every night.

To finally turn off the light.

To define absence.

To see it in every worldly shape.

To know it's something you will never escape.

SUBTRACTION

is

Logic   no   Language

A mother

(Yes

?

no   .

                    I   open
                                   violent
     language
    , try and try to

     stand   It

                                    .

I said

                dark is

A substitute for   now   :

     Now

        .

now,

mother   , unmother   .

EXILATION

My body is a clench. It blushes with hurt. But do not mistake it for a bruise. I am bright hot with pain, not color. If you want to know what part of me is indestructible, look at my hands. If you want to know what part of language is indestructible, look at what has stayed on the page.

"Increasingly," William H. Gass claimed, "to be exiled means to be sent to a place where one cannot conduct their business." But here I am, four legs of the desk sturdy on the floor, light filtering itself through the curtains down onto letters I press with the effort of work.

When someone asks me why I was exiled from my family, I don't know how to answer. My *carmen et error*, I say. Though I am nothing like Ovid and this is no *relegatio*. I have no place left in my family, nothing of my borned biological citizenship. This explanation usually garners little response. They want a concrete reason, something logical, a cause married to its effect.

Gass writes that exile nearly always involves the loss of one's language. That is why this is important.

My ability to work, to write, is my error. To tell the truth and tell it widely. Cause to its linguistic effect. I saw a bricolage of dysfunction, a family wrought with wounds passed down from generations. I resisted it, like a young child resists sleep without the comfort of their mother. I did not speak, but could, had the capacity, the tools to tell of the unspoken family rules. Here they are, silently lettered down.

The nature of any punishment is often silence. That is why this is important.

Listen: every place to me is now a floating colony and I am tethered to nothing. I skip along what feels like ground but live nowhere. I am undaughered, unsistered, unchild. In that way, I am unborn, ungestated, unimagined. Not even a glimmer of life except for these words. Can they acquire breath?

Gass wrote, "You are no longer you when even your present daily life is as remote as a memory. You are no longer you, if—especially—you were defined by your way of life, the things you loved, the ideals you esteemed, your language."

I don't know what else to say. I am all inquiry. All language now moves in me like a question. This was, once, an autotelic exercise. Now I seek no answers, only the questions that grieve them. That they are unanswerable, unsolvable, inconclusive, is just a small death.

Gass: "That you will learn a language, then, is likely; that you will learn it well is unlikely; that you will live well is unlikely; that you will have a shape is certain."

I know I have mostly failed. But finding a new life, learning a new way of living, requires new shape. A new way of staying. Here is mine: all blooming and blinking, swaddled and bedeviled, trammeled and willful and keeping, semblance of growing into its blue, little murmurs of evidence evidentiary to—

How do we know the early hominid existed? What they made survived them.

See this wall? See these tick marks? They can make a sound. You can hear them, even if you close your eyes. Close your eyes.

Now that I am pain's darling, now that I am pain's darling, now that I am pain's darling (it echoes like a song I wish were not sung) no longer does anyone, not even a lover, look at me straight in the face.

Where is the father? many have asked. The story seemingly unfinished without him. They want a fuller narrative, think a story can't be complete without shaking it loose from its hinge. Yes, father who made eight moons too. Who orbited the mother until she sent him away. There was no choice but to choose. Father who worked my childhood away. What forms of love we find suddenly in lonely offices one day.

Here is the wilderness of empty space.

[

]

The father is not there inside those brackets, not inside language, not a hero or a myth or a metaphor.

He did not rescue me from exile. He met me there and held open the door. We prop up our losses into walls, let pain cover us like a roof, and live there, together, alone.

My father and I have done our best to make this space a home.

SUFFIXATION

I write toward endings. This is why I do it. Words don't evacuate themselves.

Call it a form of truthmongering: to see something to its finality. To wonder if an end exists at all.

> (And in the room of our
> last night together,
> our bodies framed and
> breathing their answers.
> I woke as my husband
> stayed attached
> to a dream
> I waited for little flickers
> of light to spread
> across the bedpost, then
> asked him to leave)

Everything ends, I think.

Or needs ending.

See, just there, I attached a suffix to the verb "to end," *-ing*, to create a gerund, to suspend it in time: *ending*, the result in constant action.

The phenomenon of language: affix a suffix to the stem of the word, make a new word. The phenomenon is that I do not have to be its captive. That in it, there is power to transform.

> (Mother I couldn't fix, this is
> me, suffixing   you)

The suffix *-tion* is used to form abstract nouns from verbs.

> (His warm feet and back and
> large hands, brown hair swept
> across his brow, sleeping
> face: *allure, allure.*

A noun is something to take to bed
with you, then you leave it   at the door)

Suffixation is a morphological process. An inflection of ending. It sounds like *suffering*, though anything fastened does. I call it *the difficult sublime*, how we attach ourselves to things, dumbly, like mothwings.

A necessity some call *loving*.

(This is my little reverse. A dream ends so we can
live. I submit   to its darting. I married
him and did not mourn   our end, but placed
it where it had to be,
    like a permanent wall plug
    that stops a leak)

It's a formal system: to love another, to leave, to hurt. Any order works. Barthes wrote, "To speak last, 'to conclude' is to assign a destiny to everything that has been said, is to master, to possess, to absolve, to bludgeon meaning."

Armies of others couldn't.
Couldn't wait.
To suffix me.
To end me.
To end me with meaning.
To change the meaning of the end.
To repair me in meaning.
To love the end of me.

(And as soon as the mother left, I knew
that was it. What action   does:
    its overtakelessness)

Barthes: "Having attained the end of language, where it can merely repeat its last word like a scratched record, I intoxicate myself upon its affirmation."

Lover whom I've lost and resign to lose, I assign this bludgeoning not to you. Nor to what I've said.

The mother shunned me, now I *-tion* everything.

My own form of ending.

In an art museum once, the power went out but not a single person left. I swear they all walked around as if the world were lit by paint. I, myself, wanted to leave, but leaving, I thought and still do think, meant I did not believe in light.

[To dim the light, with restlessness.]

To document errors.

To know dream-logic is not a substitute for the dream.

To lean into the texture of Ohio grass.

To try and announce ecstasy.

To fold his shirts, his pants, his time, our life into threes.

To ask him to leave.

To remember you weren't always a home for pain.

To nail pain to the mantle above the fire and let it warm you.

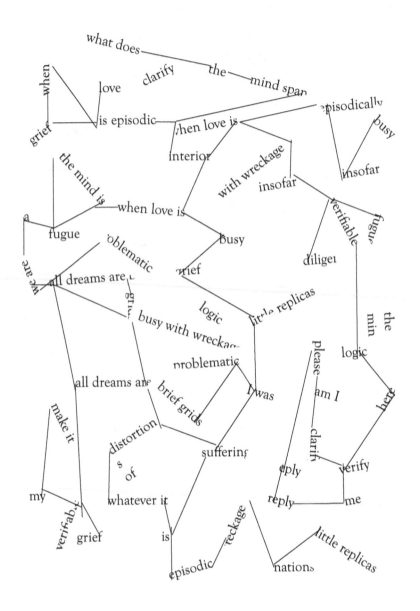

ILLUMINATION

I've carried a book with me since I was twenty-three. Its black front with two porcelain children in dull gold pressed hard against my hip. It is an image of statued figurines, posed strangely and sad. Both have no hands; they've either been erased or broken, or never part of the children at all.

Like a defiant chiaroscuro, I imagine their hands are somewhere, clutching in the dark.

In the book, the last bit of language comes after the text, after 166 pages. Under an old photograph of the author with her mother is an epitaph:

Eclipsis est pro dolore.

I've read the book one hundred times but never bothered to translate it; focusing, instead, on the immediacy of the words that come before. I didn't know how visible it could be: *the language of after*: which tells me, now, how to read *the language of before*:

The eclipse is for pain.

When I wake up, I am always about to wake. The infinitive never leaves me, even in sleep. There's something difficult—tragic even—in realizing your dreams are a world and then—there is this one.

[*To wash one's hands and brush one's teeth.*]

To stretch one's arms above the head.

To fumble with the morning tea.

To burn one's tongue five days in a row.

To dress in yesterday's clothes.

To sit down at a desk to write.

Not to earn a living but to earn a life.

To think language defies form.

To prove it.

To understand nothing but movement.

OBLITERATION

A mother can obliterate you. Now I know this.

How early ash indicates a future burning.

Once, there were fireworks in California. The Marina. My husband. A thousand others. Gold flints exploded over the smoke-lit bay. Such brightness, so quickly, then gone. The outline of faces reflected in instantaneous color. Light the fog would allow. What travels up to be made into splendor: the ignited fuse, burning salts, steel filings, heat. Hard things. There's a science in each swaying place. What travels between us. Our selves.

We had gone there—a desire for color, awe, good burning—for what can be seen in the dark. There was a concern of fire. A need for rain. What can brutalize a scape. What is left after thinking. Each fragment a statement *against*. What *Ob-* means. And *littera* for letters, something written.

OBLITERATE: to strike out a text.

I wanted it all to make sense. In the mind's mind—to remove all signs of her. A thought experiment, like Theseus's ship:

Plutarch: "... for they took away the old planks as they decayed, putting in new and stronger timber in their place, insomuch that this ship became a standing example for the logical question of things that grow; one side holding that ship remained the same, the other contending that it was not the same."

"To obliterate": a thing that no longer remains, or, to make new the form of a thing through extreme change. Can't both be true?

I had to learn how to turn away from the sky, my husband, the thousand others—from the dimming light for long enough to understand this violence.

What violet.
What soft bed.
The logic it brings.
What system of systems.
This felt life.
What suffering.
The necessity.
This advantage.
The dream.
All of the scaffolding and apple skin.
Everything that exists in between.
Every backbone.
And bridge.
Each bruised thing.

And the afterimage I've made, not from light but from language, that tells me every day:

Go on, just keep on doing what you do.

And remember to suckle the bright blue bone rain as it lashes you.

Notes

The following books and articles were used in the research and writing of this book:

Adnan, Etel. *To look at the sea is to become what one is*. Nightboat Books, 2014.

Aristotle. "Poetics." *Classic Writings on Poetry*. Edited by William Harmon. Columbia University Press, 2003, pp. 31-62.

Barthes, Roland. *Camera Lucida: Reflections on Photography*. Translated by Richard Howard. Hill & Wang (FSG), 1980

Barthes, Roland *A Lover's Discourse: Fragments*. Translated by Richard Howard. Hill & Wang (FSG), 1977

Barthes Roland, *Mourning Diary*. Translated by Richard Howard. Hill & Wang (FSG), 2009.

Brock-Broido, Lucie. *Stay Illusion: Poems*. Alfred A. Knopf, 2015.

Cage, John. *Silence: Lectures and Writings*. Marion Boyars, 1994.

Carson, Anne. "Nelligan: Some Poems translated from the French." *Float*. Alfred A. Knopf, 2016.

Carson, Anne. *Men in the Off Hours*. Vintage Books, 2000.

Caruth, Cathy. *Unclaimed Experience: Trauma, Narrative, and History*. Johns Hopkins University Press, 1996.

Celan, Paul. *Poems of Paul Celan*. Translated by Michael Hamburger, Persea Books, 2002

Courant, Richard. *What is Mathematics: An Elementary Approach to Idea and Methods*. Oxford University Press, 1996.

Dillon, Brian. "Rereading: Camera Lucida by Roland Barthes." *The Guardian*. Guardian News and Media. 3/25/2011. www.theguardian.com/books/2011/mar/26/roland-barthes-camera-lucida-rereading

Dove, Rita. *Mother Love: Poems*. W.W Norton, 1995.

Freud, Sigmund. *The Interpretation of Dreams*. Translated by James Strachey. Basic Books, 2010.

Gass, William H. "Exile." Salmagundi, no. 88/89, 1990, pp. 89–108. JSTOR, www.jstor.org/stable/40548467. Accessed 31 Mar. 2020.

Hejinian, Lyn. *Happily*. The Post-Apollo Press, 1999.

Hejinian, Lyn. *The Beginner*. Tuumba Press, 2002.

Herman, Judith. *Trauma and Recovery: The Aftermath of Violence–From Domestic Abuse to Political Terror*. Basic Books, 1992.

Lacan, Jacques. *The Four Fundamental Concepts of Psychoanalysis: The Seminar of Jacques Lacan Book XI*. Edited by Jacques-Alain Miller. Translated by Alan Sheridan. W.W. Norton, 1978.

Lee, Li-Young. *Behind My Eyes: Poems*. W.W. Norton & Company, 2009.

Lipinski, Lisa. *René Magritte and the Art of Thinking*. Routledge, 2020.

Loy, Mina. *The Lost Lunar Baedeker*: Poems. Edited by Roger L. Conover. Farrar Strauss & Giroux, 1996.

Montaigne, Michel de. *The Complete Essays*. Edited by M.A. Screech. Penguin Classics, 1993.

Mott, Gabriel. "Halation: The Single Most Important Law of Color." Web Blog Post. *Medium*. 27/1/2017.

Morrison, Toni. "The Work You Do, The Person You Are." *The New Yorker*. 06/05/2017.

Pizarnik, Alejandra. *Extracting the Stone of Madness: Poems 1962–1972*. Translated by Yvette Siegert. New Directions, 2000.

Puckett, Kent. *Narrative Theory: A Critical Introduction*. Cambridge University Press, 2016.

Robertson, Lisa. *3 Summers*. Coach House Books. Toronto, 2016.

Roubaud, Jacques. *Exchanges on Light*. Translated by Eleni Sikélianòs. La Press, 2009.

Ruefle, Mary. *Madness, Rack, and Honey: Collected Lectures*. Wave Books, 2012.

Sappho. *If Not, Winter: Fragments*. Translated Anne Carson. Vintage Books, 2003.

Scarry, Elaine. *The Body in Pain: The Making and Unmaking of the World*. Oxford University Press, 1985.

Shelley, Mary Wollstonecraft. *Frankenstein: or The Modern Prometheus*. Oxford University Press, 2008.

Sontag, Susan. *Against Interpretation and Other Essays*. Picador (FSG), 1966.

Stein, Gertrude. *Lectures in America*. Random House, 1935.

Stevens, Wallace. *The Necessary Angel: Essays on Reality and the Imagination*. Alfred A. Knopf, 1951.

Rank, Otto. *The Trauma of Birth*. Martino Fine Books, 2010.

Weil, Simone. *Waiting for God*. Translated by Kegan Paul. Routledge, 1979.

Winnicott, D.W. *Babies and Their Mother*. De Capo Lifelong Books, 1992.

Winnicott, D.W. *Playing and Reality*. 2nd ed., Routledge, 2005.

Wittgenstein, Ludwig. *Zettel*. Edited and translated by G.E.M Anscombe and G.H. von Wright. University of California Press, 1970

Wright, C.D. *The Poet, the Lion, Talking Pictures, El Farolito, a Wedding in St. Roch, the Big Box Store, the Warp in the Mirror, Spring, Midnights, Fire & All*. Copper Canyon Press, 2016.

Acknowledgments

Gratitude to the editors of these publications, where selections of this book previously appeared, sometimes in different forms:

The Adroit Journal: "Translation," "Reconjugation," "Eradication"
The Eloquent Poem Anthology: "Action"
The Kenyon Review: "Conjugation"
New England Review: "Derivation," "Devastation"
On the Seawall: "Like a carburetor, she is flooded. I wait, open choke, crank"
Plume: "I'll introduce a problem the poem can't answer: a mother," "Of vulnerability, I said the pronoun. That is the answer,"
The Rumpus: "Nonfiction," "Traumatization," "Dysfunction," "Representation," "Halation," "Deconstruction," "Imagination," "Fiction"
The Shore: "Intellectualization"
Thank you to *Lit Hub* for reprinting "Derivation," "Devastation" from NER

*

This book was written with the gracious support of Stanford University, the Civitella Ranieri Foundation, the University of Cincinnati, and The Taft Research Center. Thank you to the College of Arts and Sciences for awarding me a Dean's Dissertation Fellowship to complete this work.

To the women who loved and saved me: Hayley Zwergel Jothi, Lindsey Sosin, Chiyuma Elliott, Nicole Miner, Allison Pitinii Davis, Hannah Sanghee Park, Sakinah Hofler, Remy Steiner, Joyce Schmid, Julia Sachon, Marilyn Hilton, Maricris Hansen, Paula Stacey, Cheryl Gettleman, Jordan Durham, Andrea Scarpino, Melissa Coppola, Alexandra Teague, Dana Koster, Laura Romeyn, Jill Talbot, Sarah Perry, Maxine Patroni, Lee Hartmann, Karen Mendenhall, Dr. Vu, Kelly O'Donnell, Cara Bjornson, my late friend Etta Chinskey, and my beloved grandmother "Turtle" Diane Joy Miner.

Thank you to Jehanne Dubrow for her help with "Dispossession".

Thank you, Dr. Hans and Judith Steiner, for giving me a beautiful home to stay in, write in. To Hans, In Erinnerung, for his steadfast support. And Remy, an instant soulmate.

To my teachers: Rebecca Lindenberg, John Drury, and Jenn Glaser—who believed in this work from the beginning and gave me the time, validation, feedback, support and love I needed to complete it. I could not have written this book without you.

To Dana Prescott, Diego Mencaroni, Illaria Lochi, Spencer Reece and the rest of the Civitella Ranieri Fellows and staff who became a temporary family when I needed one most. Thank you for giving me a beautiful space in Italy, twice, to work on this book. And to Gabriel Fried for getting me there, and here.

To my peers at the University of Cincinnati, especially Madeleine Wattenberg, Chelsea Whitton, and Matthew Yeager, thank you so much for your help with this book and for being its first readers.

To all of the wonderful students I've had over the years who have inspired me with their own stories and ways to language. I take you with me through each book I write.

For E, S, and T.

Finally, for Donald Grey, who has taught me what unconditional love feels like and has made me feel, above all things, necessary. Who has worked every day of his life ("got up early/ and put his clothes on in the blueblack cold") to make sure I could do this with mine. I would not be who I am without you, your generosity, and your love. I'm saying it here where it can never be erased: you are an extraordinary father and I love you.